ASSESSMENT RECONSIDERED
Institutional Effectiveness for Student Success

ASSESSMENT RECONSIDERED
Institutional Effectiveness for Student Success

Richard P. Keeling • Andrew F. Wall
Ric Underhile • Gwendolyn J. Dungy

◆ICSSIA

International Center for Student Success & Institutional Accountability

NASPA
Student Affairs Administrators
in Higher Education

KEELING & ASSOCIATES
vision, strategy, and results in higher education

About ICSSIA

The International Center for Student Success and Institutional Accountability (ICSSIA) seeks to help postsecondary institutions worldwide improve student success and learning outcomes through professional development, applied research, and the creation and sharing of unique resources. Please visit the ICSSIA Web site at www.icssia.org

CONTENTS

CHAPTER ONE

Assessment in Higher Education: Vision and Approach

Introduction

Assessment in higher education primarily responds to two forces: external demands for accountability and internal commitments to improvement. As stewards of the public's trust (and, in most cases, regardless of institutional governance, of significant public resources), colleges and universities may be expected to provide evidence of achievement of their purposes (e.g., education, economic and workforce development, service, and research). As is true of other not-for-profit entities, this concept of public stewardship reflects a fundamental principle of organizational ethics and values—though not an uncontested one; disputes over the degree to which either public or private institutions are accountable to the public and its goals continue (Burke, 2005; Kezar et al., 2005). But the use of assessment more importantly emerges from the desire of faculty members, student affairs professionals, parents, students, and institutional administrators to know, and improve, the quality and effectiveness of higher education.

The concept of accountability has grown more complex with changes in society, broader access to higher education, rising public expectations, and the emergence of competition, positioning, and marketing among postsecondary institutions. As access to higher education increased because of the GI Bill,[1] the creation of new postsecondary systems (including the expansion of community and technical colleges[2]) that responded to different educational needs, and the gradual democratization of college admissions, public (and especially legislative) expectations of higher education began to rise (Cohen, 1998). The number and diversity of colleges and universities grew, and, eventually, the perceived need to differentiate and brand institutions by building prestige and status arose in response to market forces. The arrival of for-profit institutions, primarily for adult learners, further diversified the educational offerings available in the marketplace of higher education and created new competition for traditional not-for-profit colleges and universities. Both not-for-profit and for-profit institutions have responded to increasing consumer demand for on-line, distance, and distributed educational models. Learners have more choices, and postsecondary schools of all types have greater competitive challenges.

In response to these pressures, postsecondary institutions began to describe, explain, and position themselves in different ways with more audiences. Especially among tuition-driven institutions, self-referential factors diluted the application of an ethic of stewardship with strong competitive principles; in this environment, rankings and ratings supplanted thoughtful consideration of institutional contributions to student outcomes or social and public purposes. Most recently, attempts to standardize, benchmark, and reward institutional performance have further complicated and provoked the national dialogue on accountability; "dashboard indicators" have replaced complex, cogent concepts of accountability with instantaneous, simple expectations of compliance or satisfaction.

Left unaddressed by these developments is that second—and, we would argue, more pressing—motive for assessment: a commitment among educators and administrators *within* colleges and universities to do good work, promote student success, use resources

---

1   The Servicemembers' Readjustment Act of 1944, generally referred to as the "GI Bill," provided education and training benefits (as well as home loans) for veterans of World War II. The original act expired in 1956; at that point, more than 7.8 million veterans had participated in educational programs funded by the bill. The GI Bill was a major, pathbreaking instance of federal support for students in higher education; without question, it had a significant effect in "democratizing" college and university admissions, as well as producing a broad population of students with very different life experience than was true of then-traditional college undergraduates. This infusion of public resources not only changed the profile of students in higher education, but also added substance to the concept of public accountability.

2   The rich history of community colleges began early in the 20th century; the institution in that category, Joliet Junior College in Illinois, was founded in 1901. After passage of the GI Bill, increasing demand for more types and numbers of postsecondary institutions led to recommendations by the Truman Commission, in 1948, for the development of more community colleges. As was true of the GI Bill, these recommendations strongly linked higher education to public purposes and set the stage for public accountability.

effectively, provide a sound student experience, and serve the public good. While the consistency, depth, and sustainability of those commitments across the spectrum of faculty members, student affairs professionals, and leaders in higher education may vary substantially, it would be wrong to overlook or discount their importance.

Assessment can generate meaningful and useful results whether it is inspired by compliance with external demands or fulfillment of internal commitments; similarly, assessment prompted from any source can ask good or useless questions, collect appropriate or off-point data, and come to meaningful or distracting conclusions. The numbing lists of cross-institutional comparisons generated in response to most external forces can drain time and energy from more significant—and more often internally motivated—assessments of learning, effectiveness, and outcomes. It is unlikely that the annual rankings of colleges and universities by popular magazines have improved student learning or educational outcomes in the United States or any other nation. There is no evidence that institutions with "higher rankings" have better student outcomes—nor is there, for that matter, consensus on what those outcomes should be. And there is certainly no evidence that rankings in magazines have any relationship to the ability of institutions of higher education to serve the public good.

Assessment that responds to the requests of external audiences usually focuses on simple metrics: inputs (e.g., average pre-admission test scores or high school class ranks of entering students, the ratio of applicants to matriculated students, the number of National Merit Scholars enrolled), outputs (grade point averages, retention rates, the percentage of students who graduate within some number of years of first enrollment) and competitive factors (student satisfaction, average starting salary of graduates, ratio of faculty to students); these metrics primarily differentiate an institution from others in terms that various audiences value and can understand and document certain aspects of its operational effectiveness. But the purpose of higher education is not simply to process students through a series of stages, checking off their satisfaction of a sequence of requirements; these measures do not alone speak of the achievement of the institution's mission and goals. Operational effectiveness does not necessarily equal overall institutional effectiveness; students can pass their courses, accumulate enough credit hours to graduate, and get a degree without necessarily achieving the broad learning outcomes the institution, the public, parents, and students desire.

Assessing Learning

Primary in the mission and goals of every postsecondary institution is education itself—the process that students may experience as learning. Knowing how to assess the kind of learning that occurs in higher education is central to the ability of educators—both inside and outside the classroom, in the traditional academic faculty or in student affairs—to do their best work. The assessment of learning explores how effectively engagement with the institution increased students' ability, skill, or competency in various domains as a result of various learning experiences—a curriculum, academic major, certificate program, course, specific classroom activity, student development experience (such as leadership development), or experiential learning activity (Keeling, 2004; Keeling, 2006). Ultimately, educators need to know this: How have those elements of learning, individually or as a whole, increased students' capacity to think critically, analyze and solve problems, work with people of similar or different demographic or cultural backgrounds, lead or follow leaders, or acquire, synthesize, and apply knowledge? What transferable life skills (such as managing their own health care, participating as active citizens in the political process, or engaging in rewarding recreational and leisure activities) did students develop? Did students learn how to learn—and did they acquire commitments to lifelong learning? In other words, what difference did postsecondary education make in their lives?

Notice that these assessments of learning focus on the effectiveness of the institution, not just the ability of students to demonstrate that they have acquired or can recite new knowledge; unlike grades, which are intended to measure students' cognitive effectiveness in acquiring and applying knowledge, most assessments of the outcomes of, or changes brought about by, learning measure the effectiveness of the institution's learning environment, academic programs, and experiential learning activities in transforming students—that is, in changing their capacity, competencies, attitudes, or values (Alexander & Stark, 2003; Angelo, 2002). Higher education is not, after all, supposed to be a passive experience that leaves students untouched; on the contrary, it is supposed to make students different, to introduce new ideas, to challenge past patterns, to create intellectual discord and tension. An institution that simply moves students through its curriculum and awards them a degree has missed the entire point, and its students have been poorly served.

But the history of assessment in higher education is primarily one of exactly that: tracking students' progress toward a degree, rather than determining whether that progress is associated with any fundamental change in students. As a community of educators, we have assessed students' satisfaction with experiential learning opportunities, from leadership programs to ropes courses, and we have counted the number of students who turn out for events and activities; almost every campus health or counseling center can produce utilization data that describe the number of students in various demographic and academic categories seen during each reporting period for this or that health problem (Ewell, 2002). We are accustomed to reading reports about the number of students who live in our residence halls, are found responsible for violations of the code of conduct, or participate in certain recreational options. We have grades, credit hours, retention percentages, and graduation rates to tell us the throughput of students in the academic enterprise. But what is missing—and what the public now demands—are data that answer key, if uncomfortable questions: So what? What difference does it all make? Was it worth it?

Gathering data for input, output, and satisfaction measures is relatively easy; it seems easy to use those data to make comparisons among institutions, and most internal and external audiences can grasp the significance and implications of the metrics (higher graduation rates, greater student satisfaction, and lower faculty/student ratios are better than their contraries). But ensuring that students complete a specified number of activities or courses and catering to their need to be satisfied may not result in more skilled, thoughtful, intellectually mature students—or in more prepared, capable, and contributing citizens (hence the complaint of both graduates and employers that college did not adequately prepare them for work). The challenge to institutions of higher education has become: How do we attract, matriculate, educate, retain, and graduate learners of all ages in ways that support their emergence as intellectually mature, civically engaged, community-minded individuals; and the challenge of assessment is this: How do we know that we are successful in doing those things? At the heart of the reconsideration of assessment in higher education are those fundamental questions plus one other: Assessment for what? In other words, what purposes does assessment serve in the modern academy?

Assessment, Learning, and Higher Education Reconsidered

Assessment is a means, not an end; regardless of the cynical comments heard about assessment between sessions at conferences and in the halls of our institutions, assessment should not be done for assessment's sake. Assessment is a tool through which institutions accomplish important purposes and goals, not an empty process (Banta, 2002).

What are those purpose and goals? Assessment is a multi-stage, multi-dimensional process—a vehicle—for bringing clarity and balance to an individual activity or set of activities (Banta, 2002a). The context of higher education provides many opportunities for assessment. Indeed, assessment is integral to, perhaps even synonymous with, learning. That is, when one realizes that to learn is to make meaning of events (notice: learning is not just acquiring and applying new knowledge; it encompasses the transformative process of making meaning of that knowledge), then, the full breadth of what it means "to learn" can be understood and conceptualized. Based on that premise, to assess (which is to observe) then is the foundation of learning. Just as we ask students to make meaning—to learn—from their experiences, so too must we make meaning of *their* learning. Making meaning of how, what, when, and where students learn is a vital, exciting, and inspiring component of higher education. Assessment practice is therefore not simply a technical specialty, or a set of skills to be memorized and applied in various settings; instead, assessment work is grounded in theory and scholarship in education, the social and behavioral sciences, philosophy, and neurosciences. Our recently acquired ability to watch the brain at work—to image the process of learning itself through functional magnetic resonance imaging (fMRI)—has not only grounded our understanding of learning itself, but also set the stage for the reconsideration of assessment practice.

The need to assess learning has generated strong interest in research into the learning process itself, and, reciprocally, new knowledge of that process has generated greater interest in the assessment of learning. Fueled by the rapid flow of empirical and conceptual studies from clinicians, scientists, and scholars in the closely related fields of neuropsychology, neurophysiology, and neurophilosophy (Bennett, Dennett, Hacker, and Searle, 2007) researchers and practitioners have postulated, and then demonstrated, the essential concurrence and integration of student learning and student development, thereby highlighting the linkages of classroom and out-of-classroom learning experiences and the wholeness of student learning.

Reviewing fMRI images makes one point with extraordinary clarity: The learner matters in the learning; learners bring to educational experiences a literal state of mind—or, more accurately, perhaps, a state of brain—that deeply influences their readiness to learn and their effectiveness as learners. There is now abundant neurophysiological evidence of something that holistically-minded educators in and out of the classroom have held as an observed truth—that the probability of students' academic success, and of their transformation as people, is closely related to their personal histories, experiences, strengths, and challenges. The student whose morning was complicated by a fender bender on the way to school will learn less well than her colleague who is not distracted by worry about getting the car fixed, the adequacy of collision insurance, or how to explain the accident to others. The affective flatness of depression is experienced (and imaged on fMRI) as a lack of activation during learning experiences, as well; a student whose apathy and somber mood reduce his engagement will gain less from any learning experience, inside or outside the classroom. Institutions that are concerned about student success can no longer afford to ignore the implications of scenarios like these; it is not sufficient simply to shrug and say, "Everybody has challenges." If transformation, and not just the memorization and recitation of content, is the goal, then every institution must, as *Learning Reconsidered* (Keeling, 2004) recommended, use all of its resources in the education and preparation of the whole student.

In this formulation, the acquisition, synthesis, and application of knowledge (often, if imprecisely, called learning, or education) and student development (understood as personal and social maturation) are integrated at their core; students develop and mature as they learn about the world and themselves, which they do simultaneously (Keeling, 2004). The products, or outcomes, of learning are not, then, simply content-driven, disciplinary, or intellectual; they reflect the interaction of the learner with learning experiences and speak to the changes that occur in the crucible of higher education. This appreciation has created an international impulse to deconstruct and re-conceptualize the purpose, structure, organization, and activities of all institutions of higher education.

This inspired and necessary undoing of a traditionally segmented view of student experience (education happens in class, and development happens everywhere else) has implications for the structure of higher education. Organized in a taut geometry of strong vertical (divisions, colleges, disciplines, departments, courses, and programs) and vague horizontal (policy, administration, budget and finance, and general education) structures, most institutions of higher education do not naturally, intuitively or intentionally address the continuum of student learning across the institution and through time of enrollment. Historically, vertical elements (popularly, if tiresomely, called "silos") have overwhelmed horizontal ones (Keeling, Underhile, and Wall, 2007). This has profound implications for the assessment of student learning. To understand the impact of higher education, institutions must do comprehensive, horizontal assessment (i.e., across divisions, colleges, departments, and programs); to create (or measure) that impact, institutions must cross-link vertical programs in meaningful ways that create a continuum of learning. There is no assumption that students gain all of their new capacities, competencies, or skills in any area—such as critical thinking—from one course, or just in the major; nor do students learn everything they will come to know about leadership from the leadership development activities offered in student affairs. Overall institutional learning outcomes are exactly that—the products of students' entire engagement with every aspect of the institution (that is, with all of the resources that the institution has gathered, allocated, and integrated to support the education and preparation of the whole student). Assessing learning outcomes then requires looking at what is accomplished in many different parts of the institution, and at many different times and places during a student's enrollment; more to the point, perhaps, transformative learning—that which is being assessed—requires the collaboration of educators all across campus and the linking, interweaving, and integrating of learning experiences that occur in different ways for every student (Keeling, 2004; Keeling, 2006). It is these requirements that set the stage for redefining the priorities, roles, and partnerships of any member of the faculty or professional staff whose work is understood to be education. Almost all faculty members and student affairs professionals will fall into that category.

Educators and Assessment

Student affairs educators (often called student affairs professionals, or student life professionals) have long had as their professional mission to support personal and social maturation. While there has been some recognition that such maturation is a complex learning process, the explicit acknowledgment that learning outside the classroom is still learning (and, for that matter, that personal and social maturation—such as enhancing reflective decision-making, the ability to participate actively and comfortably in group discussions, competency in coherently expressing differences of opinion, and conflict management—in the context of courses and classrooms is still maturation) has come to be explicit only relatively recently. Many student affairs professionals have not thought of themselves as *educators*; indeed, some resist that label, preferring to understand their work as *providing excellent services*. There is, however, no conflict between providing excellent services and supporting learning; much learning occurs in the process of requesting, receiving, and understanding services.

One of the primary implications of understanding oneself professionally as an educator is the obligation to assess the learning that happens in one's programs and services. But student affairs educators and their faculty colleagues often do not have the knowledge and skills (or, often, the resources or support) necessary for engaging in the complex strategy of mapping, integrating, supporting, and assessing learning—despite their strong intuition about the opportunity for and achievement of transformation through learning experiences inside and outside the classroom. There is, however, an important difference between "haven't yet" and "can't"; the fact that the assessment of learning is relatively new in student affairs is not a prediction of failure. In fact, the opportunity to assess learning is an enormous opportunity for student affairs divisions and educators; student affairs educators can now add to their historical strengths a collective astuteness in—and commitment to—the assessment of broad student learning outcomes, and, in the process, lead the work of assessing learning in their institutions.

The same is true of most members of the academic faculty. Invested primarily in disciplinary content and accustomed to documenting learning by evaluating students' intellectual products (papers, presentations, and examinations), faculty are generally not prepared to assess the results of the integrated process of knowledge acquisition and personal development (although any conversation with a faculty member surely includes their subjective reference to the abilities or disabilities of students to fully engage in the process of learning); the usual and customary process of evaluation that results in grades does not constitute an assessment of student learning (Angelo, 2002). Learning outcomes measure change in students (what we have been calling transformation)—not the absorption, recitation, or application of content alone. Many professors protest that they already assess learning—through grades; but, in almost all cases, grades are determined by students' ability to master the content of a course, not by any larger assessment of what has changed in the students' understanding, attitudes, or perspectives. Most educators are familiar with a painful phenomenon—the student who gets terrific grades but has not really learned anything—and with a more hopeful one—the student whose ordinary grades do not accurately or adequately portray the depth and importance of his or her learning.

CHAPTER TWO

Fundamentals of Assessment in Higher Education

Assessment is the formal or informal process of observing and assigning value or worth to an event or activity. In higher education, most such events or activities are learning experiences intentionally designed and provided to promote student learning; the character, content, format, and means of delivery of those experiences varies from lectures, laboratory sessions, or group learning activities in typical academic courses to outdoor experiences, counseling visits, community service work, and peer education training outside the classroom.

Formal and Informal Processes of Assessment

Formal assessment practice includes conceptualizing, planning, implementing, and evaluating the impact, or outcomes, of a purposeful, intentional learning event on an identified set of learners (see an example in Table 1). Educators use formal assessment practices when conceiving, planning, delivering, and assessing such educational experiences. *Informal assessment* is the experience that an individual or set of individuals have when they experience an event in which learning occurs (whether or not that event was intentionally developed and designed as a learning experience by the institution) and ascribe meaning to that event (see Table 2).

Table 1. **Formal assessment.**

Topic	Assessment Stage	Assessment Activity
Men's Health Workshop Series	Identifying an educational need	Needs assessment—administering an assessment tool, such as a survey, and analyzing data that indicate the need for change in knowledge, attitude, or behaviors.
	Conceptualizing	Categorizing the identified needs; developing a scope and sequence of learning goals that illustrates who should know what, and in what general order or sequence the content should become known, as a result of the educational programming.
	Planning	Working collaboratively with others (representatives of constituent groups) to identify who or what department will create each workshop; what knowledge, skills, or attitudes students should develop as a result of the workshops (i.e., student learning outcomes); when and where each workshop will take place; how the learning opportunities will be made known to students; what assessment method will be used to determine level of impact; how assessment data will be gathered; and how that data will be analyzed, synthesized, reported, and responded to. *Note that assessment data are never collected for their own sake; assessment serves a purpose beyond assessment itself.*
	Implementing	Delivering the workshops; the format, content, and methods should respond to the learning goals, fit the learning style of the participants, and anticipate the assessment process.
	Evaluating	Developing the assessment strategy and methods; providing the assessment to the learners; gathering, analyzing, and synthesizing data; reporting findings; developing a strategy to respond to data findings; describing the data findings and proposed responses to key stakeholders.

Table 2. **Informal assessment.**

Topic	Assessment Stage	Assessment Activity
Students move into residence halls and begin to live with roommates	Identifying an education need	Students discover that they will need to know how to share space with others.
	Conceptualizing	Each student explicitly or implicitly determines how much space they will need and what their preferred space should be.
	Planning	Students make a series of decisions about how and when they will negotiate with the roommate to secure their space; these decisions include preparation for listening and responding to the needs of the roommate.
	Implementing	The student engages in dialogue with the roommate.
	Evaluating	How space will be shared is determined and each student makes meaning of the event.

The examples provided in Tables 1 and 2 illustrate important points.

First, that formal assessment is a complex process. It requires multiple steps, each with a number of options and therefore an opportunity for many decisions. To be haphazard with assessment planning is to invite an exercise in frustration.

Second, formal assessment should always be collaborative. Assessment cannot happen successfully in isolation from peers, colleagues, and the intended learners.

Third, informal assessment can have multiple outcomes. In the example of moving into a residence hall and preparing to share space with a roommate, the fact and valence of the outcome are not known. Imagine, though, if the two students lack empathy or do not have negotiation, communication, or conflict resolution skills; students in that scenario would probably be fraught with frustration, anxiety, and resentment. In contrast, if the students had empathy and strong interpersonal skills, were socially mature, and had learned to be appropriately assertive, they would have probably had a positive, even bonding, experience. The unique role and capacity of higher education is to ensure that students, in all learning situations, are offered educational opportunities to express existing skills and knowledge (in this case, the art of civility and competency in negotiation) or to seek support and learning opportunities (note that support without learning is not education, but rather merely service provision; "doing it for them" aborts the learning opportunity) from others as they strive to develop these skills in real time.

Because assessment is a complex process, it lends itself to collaborative practice. Within the context of higher education, collaborative practice usually and routinely requires participation by four common constituencies: 1) students; 2) faculty members; 3) student affairs professionals; and 4) community. In certain situations, other constituencies are also included (e.g., parents). Because assessment is inherently the determination of how students were affected and influenced by a learning event, finding a common language to describe *the holistic experience of learning* in terms and through examples that make sense to each of the primary constituencies is a foundational competency for higher education professionals.

Student Learning Outcomes

Student learning outcomes define the goals of learning experiences; they specify what a student should be able to know, do, or value after participating in those activities. There are multiple levels of learning outcomes—institutional (campuswide), divisional, departmental, programmatic, and activity-based; outcomes are written with far greater exactness and specificity at activity or program levels than at institutional or divisional levels (Banta, 2003). A university may define cognitive maturity as a broad institutional learning goal; this goal will be addressed in each division in different ways, and each division will, accordingly, state its own desired learning outcomes pertinent to cognitive maturity. A college of arts and sciences might decide that critical thinking is one of its most important desired learning outcomes within the general category of cognitive maturity; individual academic departments would address critical thinking in their own ways, and so on through the ramifications of majors, courses, and classroom activities.[1] But critical thinking is also addressed through the myriad of out-of-classroom and experiential learning experiences available to students on most campuses; the broad institutional goal of cognitive complexity, and the ability to think critically, which is an

---

1 See *Learning Reconsidered 2* (Keeling, 2006) for a complete description of learning domains and sub-domains and their application to specific programs.

essential element of that goal, will be reached by students as a result of their participation in a broad diversity of learning activities and experiences that can be mapped across their entire institutional experience (Kuh, Gonyea & Rodriguez, 2002).

Key to the concept of student learning outcomes, as to formal assessment practice, is the principle of intentionality; that is, student learning outcomes represent the desired goals of learning experiences that the institution intentionally develops, structures, delivers, and assesses. From the perspective of a college or university, students may learn unintentionally as well (through planned or accidental experiences that the institution did not design and implement); the institution cannot take responsibility or credit for those experiences and cannot meaningfully assess them, though students may themselves independently assess those experiences (through practices of informal assessment, as above) and learn from them.[2]

Theory in Assessment

The Council for the Advancement of Standards in Higher Education (CAS) advises higher education professionals to develop strategies, programs, and services based on theory (Dean, 2006). But in the literature of student affairs practice, reports of the application of theory, from conceptualization of learning experiences to their implementation and assessment, are few; it often appears that theory is the province of graduate preparation, and it yields to application and practice thereafter (Evans, Forney, & Guido-DiBrito, 1998). Many colleges and universities make statements about how constructs of human development theory are embedded in their work with students; mental health professionals often reference "brief therapy" or "client-centered" clinical approaches; physicians and psychologists describe their commitments to evidence-based or outcomes-driven practice; health educators speak convincingly of the transtheoretical model (stages of change), social cognitive theory, and brief motivational interviewing. But there is scant evidence that theory actually gets applied intentionally in day-to-day practice. Setting visit limits in a counseling center does not equate to theory-based practice according to constructs of brief therapy; evidence-based practice in clinical medicine involves more than using the next broad spectrum antibiotic that has been proven effective in some specific illness in clinical trials.

---

2   The whole of students' education during college is no longer—and probably never was—provided intentionally by the institution. Community, workplace, family, and, especially now, Internet-mediated learning experiences supplement, complement, and reinforce or undermine campus-based learning.

The pioneer of social psychology, Kurt Lewin (1951), famously wrote, "There is nothing so practical as a good theory." Like assessment, theory is not an end in itself, but rather serves, in practice, to build an essential foundation for assessment planning; assessment purposes, methods, metrics, and reporting are developed on this conceptual foundation. Planned and intentional assessment provides insight into how effectively policies, operations, programs, and services function within the context of institutional mission. Working toward a sound alignment of those complex components requires thoughtful and coherent change, and effective change is most likely to occur when each stage of assessment is consciously guided and inspired by theory.

There is, however, no one best theory—and there is no one best way to apply theory to assessment. The effective use of theory to guide comprehensive assessment planning includes consideration of staff capacity, cultural "fit" between any given theoretical approach and institutional expectations, and the ability of a candidate theory to support the achievement of desired student learning outcomes. This last point is especially important because there are different typologies of theory: to name just a few, there are individual behavior change, community or population-level change, communication, and planning theories. Each has been used to create the conditions necessary for assessing the synergistic characteristics of persons and phenomena and then nurture change. A broad variety of useful case examples from education, business, health care, and human and social services exist and can provide guidance to all campus educators.

Scholars concerned about the ways in which the college experience (in the aggregate) affects students have long considered how the person, behavior, and environment work synergistically and influence learning and development (Chickering & Reisser, 1993). Numerous recommendations about better ways to use theory creatively in understanding, mapping, and assessing development have emerged (Evans, Forney, & Guido-DiBrito, 1998). Theory has many benefits: it blends intuition with empirical knowledge, allows processes to be better understood at each stage of implementation, and can increase the strength and utility of strategic assessment planning (Glanz, 1997). Current professional literature in higher education recommends a broad institutional commitment to intentional, planned collaborative organizational change that has foundation in theory (Keeling, 2004).

Theories and Models

Theories and *models* provide frameworks within which good ideas and strategies can be supported. Theories differ from models. Theories provide "a systematic way of understanding events or situations" (U.S. Department of Health and Human Services, 2005). Theories are comprised of *concepts*, or the primary elements of the theory; *constructs*, the more specific components of a particular theory; and *variables*, the operational definitions of the constructs. Models are arrangements of theories, designed to paint a more holistic picture of the situation or phenomena being explored than any single theory would allow. Theories and models give the structure, organization, functions, activities, purposes, and effects of curricula, programs, services, and transactions meaning in relation to greater institutional mission and goals; they provide intellectual foundations that ground the work of educators securely. Unlike so-called "best practices"—which are more often than not simply the things most frequently done, or popularly endorsed— theories and models relate practices to both purposes and outcomes. Theory can be applied as a planning and guiding tool that creates a common language and framework across campus departments and programs. As a means to an end, the application of theory can lead to enhanced and more robust student learning outcomes. Subsequently, students who experience the campus as a collective, coherent learning environment that expresses cultural and developmental empathy and support are more likely to positively engage. Theory serves as a framework that can unify and streamline communication and coordination of assessment planning to better meet institutional responsibility.

Examples: Application of Theory to Assessment Practice

Theories and models can be illustrated, explored, and brought to life through examples. The case studies that follow illustrate the application of three theories; they are 1) an attempt to increase utilization of a university recreation center, which illustrates the Theory of Planned Behavior (Ajzen, 1985), 2) the development of a student affairs curriculum, which considers how principles of community organizing can be applied to a practical campus problem (Rothman, 1968), and 3) facilitating students' selection of a major through a sophomore support center, which relies upon elements of diffusion of innovation theory (Rogers, 1995). It is our experience that situations like these are ordinarily and customarily addressed in an atheoretical manner; it is our belief that using theory as a foundation will significantly improve the process and outcomes of good professional practice, including assessment, in each area.

Case study 1: Imagine that a university wants to increase students' utilization of the campus recreation center. (Of course, increasing utilization is not in and of itself a student leaning outcome, but utilization of the recreation center by students may facilitate their achievement of specific learning outcomes that are addressed by recreational programs and enhance their readiness to learn in other contexts as well.) In many (perhaps most) circumstances, recreation center staff, perhaps (but not necessarily) in collaboration with colleagues, would design a marketing and communications campaign to "get the word out" and encourage more students to use the center. Advertisements in the student newspaper, posters on easels in high traffic locations, and a special event with food and prizes might be deployed. These actions might, or might not, "work." Assessment is used to explore, and explain, the outcomes. If utilization of the recreation center increases, is it because of, in spite of, or without relation to those efforts? If utilization does not increase, why not?

In a theory-conscious environment, though, administrators and educators might desire a greater understanding of what inspires students to use the campus recreation center; they might want to know what factors in students' lives, attitudes, and beliefs are engaged in decision-making about using the recreation center. They might choose to use the Theory of Planned Behavior to assess how students choose to use (or not use) the recreation center (see Table 3). The four constructs of this theory, as applied to this question, include: 1) *behavioral intention*, which is the perceived likelihood of going to the recreation center (e.g., "Are you likely or unlikely to use the recreation center?"); 2) the student's *attitude about the behavior* (e.g., "Do you see going to the recreation center as a good, neutral, or bad thing?"); 3) the *subjective norm*, or the student's personal beliefs about whether key people in their life approve or disapprove of using the recreation center—really an assessment of the valence of external influences on the student's motivation (e.g., "Do your friends think going to the recreation center is cool or un-cool?"); and 4) the *perceived behavioral control* of getting to the recreation center (e.g., "To what extent do you have the desire and discipline to go to the recreation center?").

Table 3. **Theory of planned behavior.**

Concept	Construct	Variable
Behavioral intention	Perceived likelihood of engaging in the specified behavior	Degree of likelihood
Attitude	Students' evaluation of the specified behavior	Degree of value ascribed to the behavior
Subjective norm	Personal beliefs about how significant peers value the specified behavior	Degree of approval or disapproval students believe their significant peers would express about the behavior
Perceived behavioral control	Personal belief that one has control over engaging in the specified behavior	Degree of belief that engaging in the behavior is within one's power

In a perfect world (at least a world that is perfect for directors of student recreation centers) behavioral intention would be high, attitude would be very positive, all students would believe that their friends think going to the recreation center is quite cool, and all students would believe that they had all the self-discipline necessary for actually getting to and using the recreation center. But what if students have good intentions, good attitudes, and believe that going is cool, but fear that they won't know how to use the recreation center or its equipment? Or, what if intentions are high, attitude is good, and self-discipline is present, but students' peers think the recreation center is only for certain athletic, "jock" types? The range of answers to those questions correlates with a series of possible approaches to increasing utilization of the recreation center; every pattern of answers suggests a different set of outreach, communications, and educational interventions. A capable director would respond differently if students do not know how to use the center than if they think the center is primarily used by "jocks." Behavior theories then can guide the planning, implementation, and assessment of activities. Organizational change theories also offer a firm foundation on which to build assessment activities.

Case Study 2: In the late 1960s, efforts to influence power structures—especially those that affected (or disenfranchised) women and groups of traditionally underrepresented students—were formalized and strengthened through the development of social action and community organization theories and models. In this second case study, we explore how Rothman's community organizing theory can be applied in higher education. Rothman deconstructed the broad practice of community organizing into three categories: social action, social planning, and community development.

The purpose of *social action* is to create shifts in authority and power. In higher education, we might see social action when students protest the decisions of a senior administrator who eliminates a sports team, invites a controversial speaker to campus, or sanctions a Greek letter organization; students also exhibit social action when advocating for a diversity requirement in the curriculum, a new cultural center, or an ethnic studies program. This category of community organizing and social change is aggressive, vocal, and intentionally public; change agents depend on emotionality and media attention to provoke dramatic organizational changes. Student learning outcomes associated with this type of community organizing include the ability to identify social inequities, access and position media to provoke change, and advocate for traditionally underrepresented groups.

The second category, *social planning,* resembles expert-based facilitated change. In this model, the focus is on diagnosing and identifying a problem or deficit. This approach is typically used to address large-scale problems; it is empirical and decisive and privileges outcomes over process. Social planning relies on external experts to objectively see, understand and solve problems. Typical applications of this approach in higher education include the development and implementation of a new, diversified revenue model for the student health center to reduce the impact of a budget crisis caused by competition for or an imposed ceiling on student fee revenue; the creation of an emergency response policy for infectious disease hazards (e.g., avian flu); and the installation of message boards in campus buildings to facilitate the transmission of important safety information in the event of a campus emergency. Because this approach is expert-based, students and even department managers may play relatively passive roles in its implementation.

In higher education practice, principles of *community development* can be used to better understand how to coordinate student life programs and services—to develop a *student affairs curriculum* that has logic, scope, sequence, depth, and increasingly complex student learning outcomes. Imagine how a student affairs leadership team might inventory the array of programs and services present in the division. Using principles of community development, emphasis would be placed on inclusiveness, increasing student and staff capacity, building consensus, increasing quality of communication, and leveling power groups so that all may become constructive collaborators.

Here is an example. An early step in developing a student affairs curriculum could be to assess what student leaders perceive to be the goals and objectives—the purposes— of their clubs, programs, and organizations. We would seek to understand how student organizations function when institutions provide them basic resources and then leave them to work, start to finish, on efforts chosen, prioritized, developed, implemented, evaluated, and reported on by the student group. In this approach, an advisor (or another more experienced expert or group of advisors) is present. Student efforts and expert support are present in virtually all aspects of the work; the combined efforts define the change agent.

The next step would be to consider what developmental needs each program meets. Then, programs are arranged on a matrix that illustrates participants' year in school and developmental task, from simple to complex. After that is determined, a curriculum task force seeks to find overlaps and gaps in developmental programming. The task force then can determine how to best allocate resources to streamline and make coherent the programs offered within the division.

The anticipated learning outcomes of community development as it relates to higher education are the ability to build consensus, develop personal capacity, and engage in conflict as a means to enhance personal and group integrity. This type of organizing recognizes students as contributing assets who share each stage of the work with more experienced experts. Assessment efforts would focus on determining the extent to which those learning outcomes were achieved.

Case Study 3: In a very different way, other theorists sought to understand how individuals and communities chose to adopt or reject new ideas and practices; that effort resulted in Rogers' diffusion of innovation model. The central idea of this model has in recent years been popularized in Malcolm Gladwell's book, *The Tipping Point* (2000). Diffusion of innovation offers a set of constructs that are useful when thinking about how and why students adopt certain desired academic behaviors. Remember that an innovation only needs to be something new in any students' life—it might not be new at all in the grand scheme of things. The fact that generations of students have declared a major does not contradict the observation that choosing a major is, for any given student, the adoption of an "innovation."

An institution might wish to increase the proportion of sophomores who have chosen a major (adopted the innovation). To do this, the institution could increase support for undecided sophomores by linking academic advising with student affairs programs, such as personal counseling (for values clarification, conflict mediation, and decision support), career counseling, and learning strategies. How can diffusion of innovation theory inform this process? Diffusion of innovation theory, as applied to this question, posits that five key elements can be used to leverage support for students' decision-making when faced with the opportunity to decide educational goals in the context of choosing career paths.

Table 4 describes how each of these elements can be applied. Each element is associated with one or more questions; these questions illustrate how applying the principles of a theory can guide students to engage in more complex thinking about a very practical decision—that is, in assessing options. The third column suggests who on campus or in the community might ask those questions; this list is not intended to prescribe roles, but rather to illuminate how multiple student resources can be positioned to work with students in a coordinated way. Finally, the fourth column suggests the skills and competencies that students can gain through their engagement. These skills and competencies are drawn from multiple sources: other behavior and change theories (Prochaska & DiClemente, 1984); student development theories (Chickering and Reiser, 1993; Maslow, 1971); adolescent and youth development theories (Baumrind, 1989; Pittman & Cahill, 1992; Fetro, 1998); and cognitive theories (Bloom, 1956). This intermingling of theories also illustrates how educators from multiple disciplines can collaborate and share expertise.

Table 4. **Application of diffusion of innovation theory to choice of major.**

Element	Questions to ask	Who might ask those questions	Skill or competency-based outcome
Relative advantage	What about one course of study is better or more attractive than the current status of being undeclared?	A faculty member, residence life staff, or career counselor.	Weigh the pros and cons of committing to a course of study.
	What are the benefits of affiliating with a department or major?	An advisor within the course of study being considered by the student; another faculty member; a peer; a parent.	Formulate a rationale for and personal sense of ownership over the decision; develop autonomy.
	What are the real or perceived costs (e.g., money, time, change in schedule, etc.) of choosing a major?	A career counselor; a student already affiliated with the department under consideration.	Move from vague consideration to evidence-based decision-making.

Element	Questions to ask	Who might ask those questions	Skill or competency-based outcome
Compatibility	How consistent with the student's goals, values, and educational objectives is the considered major?	A faculty member from the department being considered; a personal or career counselor; a campus spiritual leader.	Acquire self-reflection and self-identity maturation competencies.
	To what extent will making the decision address the concerns of family members or other key people in the student's life?	A personal or career counselor; a parent, mentor, or family member.	Consider how personal decisions impact peers or family members. Move toward individuation.
	Is the potential choice of major in harmony with the student's peer reference group?	Roommates, peers, or other "key influentials" in the student's social circle.	Develop social connectivity, group belongingness, and other important characteristics that contribute to resiliency.
Complexity	How difficult is the transition from undeclared major to declared major?	Departmental advisor; personal or career counselor; a student who has recently declared a major.	Engage in critical thinking; engage in planning including time management.
	Does the student understand all prerequisites and major requirements?	Departmental advisor.	Develop critical thinking skills.
	How many new resources will be needed to make the transition (e.g., books, lab fees, equipment usage, etc).	Departmental advisor.	Make a plan that can assist in decision-making; create a budget.
	How much time and effort will be required?	Departmental advisor; peer who has declared the same major; career counselor.	Manage stress; engage in steps of decision-making; determine and set goals.

Element	Questions to ask	Who might ask those questions	Skill or competency-based outcome
Trialability	How difficult is it for the student to change majors if the choice is not a good fit?	Departmental advisor.	Think critically in order to develop a plan of action.
	How long can the student remain undeclared while taking one or two classes in the potential major?	Departmental advisor; another faculty member.	Make decisions and set goals.
	Are there opportunities for the student to meet faculty and other students in the potential major to better understand the program?	Faculty, departmental advisor, career counselor.	Develop important communication skills; learn from others about the process of career planning; develop interviewing and critical thinking skills.
	Can the student speak with graduates of the program?	Alumni officers; faculty.	Plan for an informational interview; engage in an interview; analyze and synthesize information gathered from one or more informational interviews.
Observability	To what extent will choosing a major result in tangible benefits to the student?	Career counselor. Alumni from the major being considered. Community members/ regional employers.	Plan and develop a budget that illustrates return on educational investment; compare and contrast current educational path to the one being considered; analyze and synthesize data gathered from the budget and return on investment activities.
	How much evidence is available to the student to assure her that making the decision is the best thing for her to do at this point in time?	Faculty mentor; advisor; First-Year Experience Coordinator	Engage in critical thinking; make a decision; explore how personal values may have changed and how personal goals can best be met through career choice.

Table 4 illustrates four important points:

1. The application of theory to collaborative program development and assessment of student learning outcomes is practical and can (in fact, should) be accomplished organically in the process of planning programs.

2. Theory can be used to promote the acquisition of important personal and social skills that are consistent with numerous theories and models of human development.

3. Comprehensive program planning can serve as a means of setting the stage for collaboration and the eventual development of a curricular approach to student engagement.

4. Theory can support the use of comprehensive, well-coordinated program planning that serves institutional assessment initiatives and acts as a practical strategy for increasing opportunities for undecided or deciding students to engage with a range of campus resources.

In this application of theory, students' accommodation of a community norm (declaring a major) is understood as their engagement with the five constructs listed above. Potential student learning outcomes associated with diffusion of innovation are consistent with career counseling and student development theories. Students who engage with a sophomore center that recognizes and utilizes diffusion of innovations principles could expect that they would, by working with the center, increase their capacity to engage in thoughtful decision-making, weigh the pros and cons of different career paths, and recognize how peer and family influences impact vocational aspirations.

The Value of Theory in Assessment

The use of theory to guide assessment planning adds velocity to educational endeavors. In the first case study, the Theory of Planned Behavior created a platform that could be used to assess barriers to and facilitators of students' use of a campus recreation center. The second explained how principles of community development can be applied to assess and respond to students' abilities to organize activities in student organizations. The final case study provided an example of how diffusion of innovation theory can be used to assess students' likelihood of adopting a desired change, in this case, the choice of academic major. Each case study offered a theoretical framework for linking assessment to practice.

The application of theory allows us to understand what students believe and how they make meaning of opportunities and is a necessary prerequisite to assessment planning and program development. Theory supports a better understanding of the intrapersonal, social, and motivational journeys students take as they make personal, social, and academic decisions.

Linking Assessment to Taxonomies of Learning

Following the annual convention of the American Psychological Association in 1948, Benjamin S. Bloom initiated work that would culminate in the development and publication of his Bloom's *Taxonomy of Learning Domains* (Bloom, 1956). Bloom's *Taxonomy* classifies the goals of educational experiences into three intertwined outcome domains: cognitive (mental, or intellectual, development and skills), psychomotor (manual or physical development and skills), and affective (development of feelings or new attitudes). Within each of those major domains, Bloom identified a series of learning categories that, as a sequence, specify learning tasks of increasing complexity. In the cognitive domain, for example, those categories are 1) knowledge—recall of information; 2) comprehension—understanding the meaning of a problem, and being able to state it in your own words; 3) application—applying what has been learned in novel situations; 4) analysis—dividing material into its component parts to facilitate understanding; 5) synthesis—putting parts together to form a whole, emphasizing the creation of a new meaning or structure of knowledge; and 6) evaluation—making judgments about the value of ideas and materials. Within each domain, educators might expect students to achieve learning tasks of higher complexity as they progress through the stages of higher education; what is expected of a senior, in other words, might be far greater than what a freshman would likely accomplish.

Following Bloom's initial publication (1956), he and other educators have added to this important body of educational literature (e.g., Bloom, 1975; Gronlund, 1970; Harrow, 1972; and Jonassen, Hannum, & Tessmer, 1989). Taxonomies of learning are an invaluable tool for linking assessment to learning. Taxonomies allow educators to conceptualize and map desired learning outcomes across the college experience in an orderly, meaningful manner. Effective learning outcomes, when drafted in parallel fashion to learning domains, intertwine cognitive, psychomotor, and affective competencies. Through the crafting of these complex learning outcomes, educators are challenged to consider and state exactly what impact programs should have on students—on whole students—rather than merely on students' cognition, and to specify the learning goals associated with each level of a student's progression through college.

Table 5 illustrates these concepts with an example.

Table 5. Taxonomies of student learning outcomes.

Domain: Citizenship			
	Cognitive	**Psychomotor**	**Affective**
First-year students	Define what it means to be a campus student leader.	Demonstrate how to constructively facilitate a class discussion.	Awareness of how interpersonal skills express basic social competencies like respect, cooperation, and patience.
Sophomores	Explain why interpersonal skills are core elements of citizenship.	Engage in conflict mediation through student organizations, classroom discussions, or debate.	Distinguish levels of citizen advocacy like activism, radical activism, and civil disobedience.
Juniors	Apply principles of civility when faced with peer pressure (e.g., setting boundaries, engaging refusal skills, and clear communication).	Assist first-year and sophomore students in values clarification activities, both formally (in student organization activities) and informally (in residence halls, service learning activities, or alternative spring break experiences).	Describe one's personal sense of integrity.
Senior	Describe and discuss characteristics of citizenship and incorporate those into campus leadership programs.	Analyze leadership portfolios of first-year student scholarship applicants.	Assist college administrators by synthesizing student leaders' accomplishments and creating an annual report.

Table 5 illustrates how students can develop complex, yet practical life-long skills and competencies through coordinated, planned, sequential learning outcomes. Further, this example clarifies how student learning outcomes are a vehicle for gathering data.

Learning taxonomies, then, are not an abstract exercise assigned to staff and faculty, but rather a set of expectations that inform students about campus expectations, including how accomplishment of those expectations will be determined. Students then are offered respectful opportunities for learning as whole people—not simply handed pages of policies and rules or directed to Web sites that define the hierarchy of violations of the student code of conduct.

While student affairs professionals and other educators may intuitively understand and experience the developmental progression of students' cognitive, personal, and social maturation, using a taxonomy of learning adds a much needed strategy for ensuring intentionality in inspiring and supporting student learning. It is through the development of a unique learning taxonomy that each institution discovers how its specific set of intentions and desires for students can inspire more cogent and meaningful curricula, courses, programs and services. For example, a college that has a strong affiliation with Benedictine tradition will design a learning taxonomy that differs from yet would complement a taxonomy that finds its roots in Dominican tradition. A university that promotes research as a vital strategy for life-long learning will conceptualize and promote the process of student learning differently than does one that primarily advocates for students' development of competencies for life-long citizenship. To some extent, all colleges and universities seek to instill common competencies in students—but there are essential differences in emphasis, sequence, methods, and context. In institutions of any type, the rationale for and prioritization of learning outcomes links mission to practice. And that is the fundamental purpose of assessment.

Early professional development efforts designed to increase educators' capacity to prepare student learning outcomes and develop appropriate assessment plans sometimes (mistakenly) proposed a template or standardized process. While the principles of assessment planning are reasonably generalizable across higher education, the expression of student learning should and must resonate with the unique culture, mission, context, and values of each institution, which can be expressed succinctly through the institution's learning taxonomy. Professional development and training programs for the development and assessment of student learning outcomes must inevitably then be customized to meet the needs of each institution and its faculty and student affairs professionals.

Developing a scope and sequence chart—which is derived from an understanding of the taxonomy of learning—can bring clarity and unity to assessment planning. A scope and sequence chart illustrates how student learning outcomes become increasingly complex over time, what program or service will promote each unique student learning outcome, and at what point in time a particular program or service should be offered. Through this framework students can be guided and advised through their higher education experience in a way that allows them the greatest opportunity for making meaning. Further, the development of a scope and sequence chart instills a sense of shared ownership and spirit of collaboration among educators. It also provides a reference tool that orients veteran and novice faculty and staff to a common structure. Ultimately, a scope and sequence chart arranges and documents each institution's own taxonomy of learning; it is the practical expression of that taxonomy.

Assessment in Political Context

Political pressures (whether generated within higher education or from sources external to colleges and universities) have forced higher education, as a community, into a defensive position, in which it is all to easy to subscribe to the mistaken view that assessment is more about "proving" or justifying than improving. As is true of evaluation, assessment seeks data that lead to the improvement of all intentional learning experiences (Davis, 2003). In doing so, assessment stands in clear contrast to research, which is a strategy to *prove* (or disprove) something (Stufflebeam & Shinkfield 1985). Assessment, unlike research, does not set out to test hypotheses, but, instead, strives to know, and document what is; the data gathered through assessment activities then inform efforts to change what is.

Assessment, as a strategic process and a powerful means of promoting transparency, carries political force; with that force comes the opportunity for demonstrating accountability. Transparency, political force, and accountability each individually and together offer myriad opportunities for educators to promote understanding, support, and positive rapport with multiple constituencies. *Transparency* informs the public—multiple stakeholders including parents, current and future students, alumni, governing boards, and community members—of how the institution engages students in holistic learning. Beyond simple and popular metrics, the transparency of assessment activities that document learning explains thoughtful, cogent, linked programs and their outcomes— those that offer academic credit and those that do not. *Political force* is the expression of the institution's integrity; it shows good will and organizational citizenry, and is the core of institutional credibility. *Accountability* knits together political force and transparency. It allows stakeholders to understand how programs came about, what their purposes are, what skills and competencies they seek to instill in students, and what learning outcomes have been developed through those programs (Ewell, 2005). Accountability is a proactive strategy for sharing the reasons for and results of the institution's efforts with audiences who seek to understand how the institution works, what it does, and what it accomplishes. Transparency, political force, and accountability, whether taken individually or as an integrated triad, strengthen perceptions of higher education and, in the process, educate the public about the true purposes of higher education.

The Role of Assessment in Higher Education in Promoting the Public Good

Throughout this monograph, we emphasize the essential role of assessment in supporting the ongoing, dynamic efforts of colleges and universities to educate the public about the purposes, roles, functions, and outcomes of higher education (Burke, 2005b). Postsecondary institutions of all types and at all levels have been coerced into (but, candidly, also have too often collaborated in) limiting the national dialogue about the value and outcomes of higher education to uncontextualized, disconnected reports of popular, but largely uninformative metrics, such as test scores, graduation rates, and student satisfaction (see Chapter 1). While each of these measures has some significance, neither individually nor in the aggregate do they effectively or meaningfully portray the breadth of purpose of educational institutions. Colleges were not organized simply to give students grades, retain them in school, or provide credentials.

Just as access to higher education has become a broad expectation and not a limited social privilege, accountability now responds both to the demands of funding committees in state legislatures, and more generally to the public's "right to know." Assessment in higher education can serve as a much-needed strategy through which colleges and universities can address their responsibility for promoting the public good (Ramaley, 2005). Higher education offers learners of all ages with the entire range of educational purposes (there are no longer accurate divisions or distinctions between "adult learners," "non-traditional students," and traditional age undergraduates—learners of all ages commingle in community colleges, public and private colleges and universities, not-for-profit and for-profit institutions, and virtual learning environments) scores of opportunities to develop content knowledge, personal and social skills, and lifelong competencies in citizenship. Any of these educational options can promote the public good by increasing the overall capacity of the citizenry; the level of degree attainment is positively correlated with health status and annual income. When institutions of higher education effectively promote deep learning, current and graduated students will strengthen the workforce, promote greater economic development, contribute to a higher community standard of living, demonstrate and support a variety of civic engagements, and become lifelong learners—all consequences that redound to the public good. Assessment is the primary means through which higher education can ensure that those positive outcomes for their students—and, therefore, for society—occur as predictably and universally as possible. Although too many past efforts have promoted assessment as an *ad hoc* activity reluctantly accepted as a matter of satisfying external requirements, rigorous, organic assessment can and should serve as a constant mirror in which the institution and its constituents observe how well the institution is functioning (Gray, 2002; Messick, 2003).

Using Assessment to Support Curriculum Development, Student Learning, and Institutional Effectiveness

The curriculum in an institution of higher education is the blueprint from which educators design learning experiences. Curriculum development is a tool for weaving together all the intricate and infinitely complex opportunities for student learning, reflective practice, and intellectual discourse that comprise that blueprint. Curriculum development, when combined with assessment, supports institutional effectiveness; colleges and universities can use assessment findings to support the continual development of fresh, practical, and challenging curricula that reach into "every nook and cranny" of the institution (Whitt, 1999).

Curriculum development, approached as a way to identify and marshal all institutional resources to support learning, supports collaborative action among student affairs educators, faculty members, and administrators (Palomba, 2002). Effective curricula should challenge students beyond the acquisition of knowledge. Curricula should inspire and perturb, prompting students of all ages to reconsider their ideas, beliefs, behaviors, relationships, and culture. The essence of postsecondary education is growth and change. The curriculum defines the set of organized experiences that foster individual growth, reflection and reconsideration, and change (all of which is what is captured in the term "transformative learning"). When students complete any of those experiences, they should somehow emerge with different perspectives rooted in the development of new, or renewed, meaning. The intentionality in "somehow" is provided through the curriculum. The curriculum blends developmental and academic opportunities to create transformative potential for learners. But in most colleges and universities, curriculum development, like assessment, has been fractured into multiple components that match the primarily vertical organization of institutions (Keeling, Underhile, & Wall, 2007). The crafting of trans-divisional—and, indeed, pan-institutional—curriculum development and assessment strategies can result in a new, more coherent paradigm of higher education (Mentkowski & Loacker, 2002; Sell, 2003).

Assessment is a strategy to support curriculum development, student learning, and institutional effectiveness (Black & Kline, 2002). Higher education professionals must think beyond assessment as a set of activities (which it includes), and toward the conceptual guidance that assessment provides. When assessment is performed effectively, it has these fundamental purposes, characteristics, and uses:

Fidelity to mission/institutional identity: The purpose of assessment is fully institutionalized; trans-divisional collaborations and divisional, departmental, and programmatic efforts are conducted within the context of the institution's mission and vision; the unique qualities of the institution are expressed in the choice of learning domains, sub-domains, student learning outcomes, data gathering strategies, and responses to data; the data are synthesized in a way that allow them to express an intricate narrative that affirms the good will of the institution.

Developmental pertinence (resonance/relevance): The way that assessment is approached is curricular, with emphasis on developing student learning outcomes that meet the cognitive, affective, interpersonal, intrapersonal, and cultural needs of the students whom the institution wishes to serve; assessment is conceptualized as and crafted to continually challenge students to think critically, gain reflective skills, and contribute to the overall quality of the institution; student learning outcomes are sequenced to become, over the duration of students' college career, increasingly complex; the accomplishment of student learning results in intellectually and socially mature learners; learning and the assessment of learning have temporal meaning to learners and educators—assessment builds a bridge between learners and educators so that each understands self and one another in a more authentic way.

Holistic: Assessment informs and enlivens curriculum development, student maturation, and overall institutional effectiveness by responding to the assets and needs of all students. Assessment is a guiding principle, used as the basis for questioning the need for, worth of, and impact of student life programs, academic experiences, and infrastructure (e.g., admissions, retention services, financial aid, military programs, etc); comprehensive assessment results, including outcomes data, bring coherence and unity to daily work and the student experience.

Linked to professional development activities for faculty, staff, and administrators: The institution's leadership guides, supports and participates in planned, sequential, institutionally relevant learning activities that instill skills in faculty and staff necessary for creating substantive change in learners (O'Banion, 1999). In collaboration with those charged with assessment activities, the institution makes available to staff and faculty workshops, seminars, and individual coaching designed to help them enhance the learning experiences of students; a recognition and reward system is in place to honor the commitment of faculty and staff as they engage in their personal student learning portfolios. This learning institute approach proactively conceptualizes, develops, implements, and assesses the impact of professional development; it serves as an organizational reflection tool.

Building community capacity: The general public should be regularly provided news and information that illustrates how the institution accomplishes its learning mission; knowledge of the purpose, practice, and outcomes of assessment data should be shared via news releases, the institution's Web site, community forums, and in state, regional, national, and international professional association events; the community should be able to differentiate output data (e.g., basic quantitative descriptions of student population, graduation rates, administrator's salaries, etc.) from purpose information (e.g., What is assessment? What functions does a provost facilitate? A dean? How is external funding determined for the institution?) and outcomes data (e.g., What are the skills and competencies that students are gaining? How prepared are they when they enter the learning experience? Through what strategies does the institution strive to instill critical thinking in students? or What is the nature of faculty/staff collaboration?).

Summary

The elucidation of formal and informal assessment underscores the complexity of meaning making and the necessity of collaboration to better observe how and through what means students develop skills and competencies. Guiding student learning allows students to develop—to change—and the practice of crafting student learning outcomes blends intuition with theory. Using theoretical constructs and principles brings intentionality to assessment practice. That intentionality, in turn, sets the stage for active collaboration. Together, theory and intentionality create a frame in the curriculum that supports the integration of learning experiences (horizontality, as it were) and enhances institutional flexibility, velocity, and resiliency.

Of course, all of this happens in the context of public accountability. Embracing the political context of assessment liberates educators. Transparency, political force, and accountability then are understood as institutional expressions of good will and integrity. Colleges and universities, in all their complexities and forms, offer myriad benefits to their nearby and distant communities. Using assessment to support curriculum development, student learning, and institutional effectiveness allows postsecondary education to inspire and inform not only its enrolled learners, but also the communities it serves.

CHAPTER THREE

Rigor in Assessment

Acommon concern in the development and implementation of assessment plans and their accompanying activities is ensuring *rigor*. Rigor describes the processes put in place so that the educational processes for supporting and accomplishing student learning, defining desired learning outcomes, identifying and collecting data, and determining and analyzing results are each and all credible. Common terms associated with rigor are: reliability, validity, objectivity, generalizability, trustworthiness, transferability, dependability, and confirmability (Isaac & Michael 1997; Pike, 2002; Lincoln & Guba, 2003). Rigor qualifies the evidence collected to show that programs—in process and content—are conceived intentionally, planned carefully, and implemented thoughtfully and effectively.

Rigor in Assessment and Research

Gathering data about the achievement of student learning outcomes, analyzing those data to formulate findings and results, and disseminating the results are of little practical use if the data are not credible, the analysis is haphazard, or the presentation of results fails to resonate with observers and critics who whose support is necessary for institutional sustainability. Although the assumptions and purposes of assessment and research are different (see Chapter 2), the demand for rigor in assessment responds to the same need for credibility that motivates insistence on rigor in research (Messick, 2003). Determining rigor in educational outcomes necessarily differs from defining rigor in research; what is necessary to establish the trustworthiness of results that *prove* or *disprove* something (i.e., research) is different from what is necessary to demonstrate the credibility of results that *document* observations of something (Gardner, 2003).

Although rigor in assessment differs from that required in research, it borrows from the principles of rigor in research. The objective of the assessment of student learning is documenting the accomplishments of the curriculum itself—the program of learning experiences intentionally designed and developed to achieve the institution's desired student learning outcomes. Institutions that are just beginning their assessment work may assess only one or two programs in the curriculum; colleges and universities that have a more mature, embedded assessment program may assess the entire range of courses and programs embraced by the curriculum that offer learning experiences inside or outside the classroom (please refer to Chapter 2 for a full discussion of the essential integration of assessment and curriculum development). Regardless of the extent of assessment, it comprises *documentation*; in contrast, the objective of research is the testing of hypotheses—research subjects an idea (the hypothesis) to empirical scrutiny. While assessment reports on the observation of change, research reports on the degree of correlation or causation among variables. With that said, advanced assessment practice can, and should, often include research as an integrated, high-level component of comprehensive assessment (Palomba & Banta, 1999).

Rigor in assessment is heavily influenced by the theories, practices, and standards of qualitative research and evaluation, because of the emphasis on *observation* present in the assessment of student learning (Lincoln & Guba, 2003; Madaus, Stufflebeam & Scriven, 2003). Learning is a complex activity that manifests its effects in some sort of change—thus the emphasis on examining what students should be able to "do, know, or value" after their engagement with learning experiences. Note that assessment practice must be comfortable with saying "after" as well as "as a result of" learning experiences; assessment is more concerned with where students end up than where they started, and it is more interested in results than ways and means. Unlike research, assessment does not need to *prove* that a certain learning experience alone produced a certain learning outcome—only that students who completed that learning activity had, at the end of it, the desired competency.

Questions of rigor then must resonate with *reflexivity*, or the realization that the observer is an integral component of the learning experience (Altheide & Johnson 1998). Assessment strategies often include interviews, review of portfolios, observation of an actual activity, students' self-reports through journaling or blogging, and other types of narrative data gathering. Assessment practitioners must have strong skills and competencies in creating, implementing, and reviewing these types of data gathering tools. To do assessment of learning outcomes, educators must be familiar with rubrics and narratives as much as, or more than, statistics and research study designs. Gone are the days of "this is easy"; rigorous assessment requires all campus educators to engage fully in the training and professional development necessary for producing credible assessment data (Sewall & Smith, 2003). As any competent researcher knows, sound qualitative inquiry is as demanding and rigorous as quantitative investigations.

Developing Sound Assessment Questions to Guide Inquiry in Practice

All educators should adhere to sound principles of practice—from beginning to end—when engaging in assessment practice (Palomba & Banta, 1999). Conceptually, educators must consider exactly what is to be explored, better understood, retained, improved, or discarded by engaging in assessment practice. Key questions to ask include:

1. What should students at this institution be able to do, know, or value as a result of their engagement with our particular form of higher education? How do the values, principles, context, and history of our institution inform those goals? How do they reflect our current institutional mission?

2. How should students' knowledge, skills, or values be changed, reinforced, or enhanced over the duration of their educational experience here? What do we expect of them at each level of their engagement with our learning community?

3. How should programs, services, and systems of support be aligned and integrated to best meet the learning and developmental goals and needs of our students?

4. What criteria will determine ample accomplishment of student learning for each program; what level of accomplishment determines program success? At what level of accomplishment would we determine that a program requires substantial revision, reconsideration, or retirement?

5. What learning strategies will best link the curriculum and its associated student learning objectives to outcomes? That is, how do we translate our educational goals into classroom and experiential learning experiences that will enable students to succeed?

6. What are the best data gathering methods for assessing the effectiveness of our learning programs in supporting student learning? How might those methods vary across the spectrum of learning experiences offered on our campus?

7. What resources exist or could be allocated to support data gathering, analysis, synthesis, and dissemination?

8. With whom will the assessment data, analysis, and results be shared? Through what means? And by whom?

9. What is our programmatic, departmental, divisional, and institutional capacity for change? To what extent does tradition impede change? How does concern about possible change create resistance to assessment? How might that resistance be understood and ameliorated?

10. What are the professional skills, competencies, aptitudes, and capacities of educators on our campus to fully engage in assessment planning? How can staff and faculty best be linked or partnered to do their best work? What professional development needs exist? How will they be met? What resources exist to support those activities? (See Chapter 5 for a detailed review of these questions.)

Promoting Rigor in Assessment

Rigor in assessment is important because of the necessity for the practice of assessment to be credible in responding to internal and external information needs. Information needs sometimes appear in the form of calls for accountability, but also are essential for ensuring improvement processes, providing information for decision making, and ensuring that the espoused values of higher education are being put into action. But espousing an off-the-shelf set of criteria for quality in assessment too quickly devolves into support for assessment practice that is mechanistic, and even mindless; "one size fits all" assessment plans fall apart when applied in different institutional contexts and fail to enhance the work of educators and assessment professionals. Instead, we propose these categories for consideration in advancing rigorous assessment practice that strives toward credibility and trustworthiness with both internal and external stakeholders.

1. **Assessment practice should be transparent.** A first category of rigor in assessment is that assessment is transparent—that is, that the purpose, value, stance, and use of assessment are shared openly in the planning, implementation, analysis, reporting and use of results.

   a. The purpose of a given assessment effort should be made very clear. Whether an effort is intended to develop information to improve an institution, judge the quality or effectiveness of a program, or develop new knowledge, that purpose of an assessment must be directly specified and openly shared.

   b. The values underpinning the inquiry must also be clear. Making values transparent can include ensuring that diverse voices are heard in the assessment process, seeking and attending to the input of traditionally marginalized persons, developing a process that ensures equal voice in the assessment for individuals at different levels of organizational power and influence, or maintaining a posture of detached neutrality.

   c. The position or stance from which an inquirer approaches the assessment should be articulated. Whether the inquirer is friendly, critical, detached, or striving for an unbiased approach, that stance, or posture, should be discussed and illuminated. Clarifying the stance of the inquirer provides an opportunity to surface and resolve or highlight organizational conflicts of interest.

   d. The intended use of an assessment effort should be articulated from the outset, so stakeholders can understand the context in which information is being gathered and toward what end it will be employed. Especially, there should be an expressed, articulated commitment to utilize assessment information, given the time, intellectual effort, energy, and resources required for any assessment process.

2. **Assessment should engage stakeholders.** Assessment is a process that is done *with* and *among* students, staff, administrators and faculty, not an action done *to* them. Assessment should intentionally, visibly,

and forthrightly engage stakeholders in the process of inquiry (Palomba & Banta, 2003).

3. **Method should respond to question and context.** Assessment, as applied inquiry, should be driven by questions and context, not by some *a priori* orientation toward a specific method. Stakeholders (and inquirers) may have an orientation toward certain methods; that orientation may comprise a significant bias about what type of evidence will be seen as credible. Ultimately, it is the context and questions to be answered through the assessment that should drive the selection of methods.

4. **Assessment should strive to adhere to the tradition of each employed method.** While rigor should not be defined as rigid adherence to methodological tradition, it is essential that criteria for rigorous inquiry within any methodological tradition be respected and adhered to as much as is contextually possible. Qualitative, quantitative or mixed methods processes should be conducted ways that adhere to the highest possible standards.

5. **Assessment should be ethical.** Assessment inquiries must protect human subjects, attend to open and honest reporting, and be conducted in accordance with applicable ethical guidelines (see the Joint Committee Standards on Educational Evaluation, 1994 [accessible at www.eval.org] as one example of ethical guides for applied inquiry).

6. **Assessment should attend to questions of the public good.** Assessment should do more than provide information in answer to internal or external requests—it should respond to questions of practical philosophy, i.e., is what higher education doing good for society (Schwandt, 1996)? Assessment has an important role in helping society take stock of the direction of the enterprise of higher education and its effectiveness in serving the broad, if somehow abstract, public good—not just in economic terms, but in relation to overarching social and democratic goals (Greenwood & Levin, 2003).

Summary

Ensuring rigor in assessment increases the real and perceived credibility and value of the process and outcomes of assessment efforts. Principles of assessment are similar to those of research methods. However, while research seeks to prove or disprove stated hypotheses, assessment seeks to elucidate how, under what circumstances, and to what extent a phenomenon (like learning) occurs. So, while the principles are similar, their application is different. Understanding the characteristics, requirements, and parameters of rigor increases the overall quality of assessment practice. Because rigor in assessment is a vital and necessary component, leaders, managers, and practitioners must fully invest in professional development that increases their conceptual and practical competencies. Finally, assessment practice should be transparent, engage stakeholders, create and respond to questions and context, reflect the tradition of the employed method, be ethical, and sustain the implied compact between higher education and the public.

CHAPTER FOUR

Methods and Innovation in Assessment Practice

Innovation in assessment seeks to blend methods of observation, documentation, measurement, and analysis to support rich, robust assessment activities and results that attend to and capture the diversity of the student experience. In this chapter, we explore core concepts of quantitative and qualitative inquiry that inform strong assessment practice, using those concepts to identify opportunities for innovation in assessment in higher education. Educators who value and practice innovation in their assessment work are, by definition, scholar–practitioners; their efforts are inevitably and essentially driven by scholarship and supported by strong preparation and ongoing learning.

Process and Outcome in Assessment Practice

The work of assessment in practice engages questions of both process and outcome. Scriven (1976) drew a distinction between process and outcome in applied inquiry by noting that knowing how a program functions (process) is different from knowing what was produced by a program (outcome). Assessment of process in higher education is important as it ensures that the gathering of data tells the story of how activities, be they courses, programs, or policies, function within an institution. Process data tells an important part of the story of an institution—as examples, the average SAT of entering students; a thick, rich description of what it is like to be a student at an historically black college; and how satisfied students are with institutional educational opportunities. Process is essential to understanding how the university is functioning, just as outcome examination is vital to answering questions of how students have changed. The perplexing challenge of outcomes assessment efforts in higher education relates to questions of attribution, or whether changes in individual learning can be attributed to particular educational experiences (see discussion in Chapter 3). Discerning whether change is genuinely attributable to university engagement or to other external forces is a major challenge in the assessment of higher education. That challenge pushes assessment practice to develop evidence of outcomes while making reserved and limited statements of attribution.

Quantitative Methods in Assessment

The use of quantitative assessment methods in higher education is common; there are volumes of information to inform scholar–practitioners about their use (Agresti & Finlay, 1997; Gall, Gall & Borg, 2003; Kuzma & Bohnenblust, 2001, Lee, 2003; Posavac & Carey, 1997). The description here is intended to identify the specific perceived value of quantitative information, highlight four types of quantitative assessment information commonly utilized in higher education, and identify five general quantitative competencies necessary in assessment practice.

The Value of Quantitative Information

The value of quantitative approaches in higher education is often seen in the perceived *economy, generalizability, reliability,* and *validity* of measures. The perceived *economy* of quantitative approaches derives from a positive view of both the time and resources required to gather quantitative data; while this does not always hold true, with modern technology it is possible for quantitative test and survey data to be gathered and analyzed rapidly at a relatively low cost. The advent of easy to use on-line survey tools provides strong support for that view. The push toward quantitative data often arises from the allure of being able to quickly and easily gather information that will be perceived to be valid. The challenge is that quantitative data are only as good as the quality of the data gathering process by which they are generated. Processes that use tools that are systematically developed, validated, and administered in a manner designed to produce representative results are far more expensive than basic survey gathering strategies, which may be of far lesser quality and certainly gather less robust information.

Another dimension of the perceived economy of quantitative assessment data is the ability of many quantitative tools (surveys, especially) to report data in consistent, attractive, and quick to consume formats. Executive summaries of quantitative data provide useful snapshots of findings that can inform administrative action. Of course, as in all inquiry, understanding the details and nuances of quantitative data requires more than an executive summary; the attractive reports of quantitative data run the risk of oversimplification.

Good quantitative data are gathered in ways that ensure that the responses of a portion (sample) of a group (population) can represent, or be *generalizable* to, the whole group. Gathering information from a sample and extrapolating findings to a group is a central premise of quantitative data gathering. Institutional leaders always want to be confident that the data on which they are basing important decisions is representative. *Generalizability* supports the *economy* of quantitative methods; since it is not practical to ask every student their views, a sample of students can be asked, and the responses of that sample can be understood to be representative of those that might be obtained from all students.

Reliability and *validity* are other important perceived benefits of quantitative data. The well-articulated techniques (processes or methods) of quantitative inquiry, whether in instrument design (survey or test), administration, analysis, or reporting, allow for the application of commonly understood criteria that define quality. The criteria for rigor in quantitative assessment are very similar to those used to define rigor in quantitative research—criteria such as random sampling, response rates, replicatability, internal validity, and precise analytic procedures (i.e., measures of central tendency and inferential statistics). Discerning the quality of quantitative information, in other words, is based upon a set of criteria that are well documented. Questions of whether quantitative assessment information is valid and reliable can be answered based upon a determination of the adherence of the process to known and reproducible techniques (Gall, Gall & Borg, 2003).

Known criteria of quality, and the perception that quantitative assessment efforts may be less influenced by observer or inquirer bias, also create political value for quantitative data. Data that are perceived by internal and external stakeholders to be valid and reliable can be a powerful tool in making one's case, or telling an institution's performance story. Indeed the attraction of quantitative data is that they have political power because of their economy, generalizability, and perceived reliability and validity.

Categories of Quantitative Data

There are at least four categories of quantitative data with which educators and administrators engaged in assessment should be familar. The categories as conceived and presented here are not mutually exclusive, but rather interrelate; they include:

1. **Institutional indicators.** This type of data is commonly collected by offices of institutional research and comprises reports on enrollment counts, faculty numbers and activities, finances, and graduation and retention rates. Data of this type are often reported to state and federal governments and then become a matter of public record; as examples, consider campus crime statistics and the large set of annual data submitted by all institutions to the Department of Education through the National Center for Educational Statistics. A vast array of information related to students and faculty is publicly available through the Integrated Postsecondary Data System (IPEDS), including, for example, the race and ethnicity of students attending an institution, faculty to student ratios, tuition cost, average faculty salary (by rank), and an institution's 6-year graduation rate. Institutional indicator data are also commonly used for and available through college rankings offered by major publishers.

2. **Test and grading data.** Data from ACT, SAT, MCAT, GRE, other pre-admission tests, and subject or discipline specific tests are unique sets of information common to institutions of higher education. Student examination scores and grade point averages (GPA) are often utilized as an expedient set of measures of student capability or performance. Test data measure standard (certain desired level of knowledge) or normative (comparative set of knowledge to like peers) knowledge, while grades are intended to reflect performance in specific courses.

3. **Large survey data.** Higher education is fertile ground for large surveys. These are highly developed surveys given to students across multiple institutions. There are major survey efforts conducted to provide information that is representative of college students generally, from the National Center for Educational Statistics (the National Educational Longitudinal Survey, or the Baccalaureate and Beyond Survey, as examples); there are also national surveys designed to be representative of institutions, such as the College Learning Assessment (CLA), the Cooperative Institutional Research Program (CIRP) freshman survey, the

National Survey of Student Engagement (NSSE), the CORE survey of alcohol behaviors, the National College Health Assessment (NCHA), or the surveys of members of professional organizations in higher education (such as counseling center directors or housing officers). These large survey efforts are supported by not-for-profit or for-profit organizations that develop them and then assist institutions in implementing the surveys and analyzing their results. Often (but not always), these surveys produce data that can be compared between institutions.

4. **Local survey data.** With the advancement of computer software applications that facilitate survey design and administration, statistical analysis, or reporting, locally implemented survey efforts have become a common way to gather quantitative information (Borden, 2002; Shermis & Daniels, 2002). Whether a survey is systematically designed for yearly administration or developed to gather information about a specific event, surveys conducted on the institutional level now supplement—and sometimes have replaced—other means of quantitative data-gathering.

Competency in Collecting and Interpreting Quantitative Data

One of the great challenges inherent in using quantitative data is ensuring that inquirers and observers have the basic skills needed to meaningfully interpret the vast array of numeric information that can be made available in higher education. There are five core competencies necessary for the consumption and utilization of quantitative information.

1. **Foundational thinking regarding quantitative inquiry.** Quantitative assessment is based upon the assumption that numbers can meaningfully represent the social world. Quantitative assessment is founded on the idea of reduction—that a number, such as a test score, accurately and meaningfully represents a level of knowledge.

2. **Sampling and Populations.** Quantitative assessment relies on the idea of asking part, or all of population, to respond to questions that are numerically coded. The proper identification of what comprises a population and the reliable determination of how a sample is drawn from that population are central requirements of quantitative methodology. There are multiple approaches to sampling (simple random, clustered random, convenience, intentional, etc.) that have different implications for the ability and trustworthiness of a sample to accurately represent a larger population.

3. **Different study designs and purposes.** There are multiple types of study designs that have different purposes. This is to say that not all quantitative data gathering strategies are the same or equal. Surveys can be cross-sectional, panel, or longitudinal, and can be delivered in an experimental, quasi-experimental, or non-experimental fashion. At minimum, persons who participate in or use quantitative results should know how, and why, different study designs have different purposes and implications.

4. **Descriptive measures and the meaning of inferential statistics.** Examination of quantitative assessment data requires an understanding of basic descriptive and inferential statistics. Descriptive statistics are measures of central tendency of the data, such as mean, median, mode, and standard deviation. Inferential statistics are intended to examine the extent to which data from a sample are representative of a population.

5. **Basic understanding of what makes a good survey.** Understanding basic survey design includes: a) knowing the key characteristics of a good survey question, b) the ability to develop basic response metrics, c) the ability to articulate how question placement and survey length affect response rates, and d) a basic comprehension of survey administration procedures that both protect human subjects and are more likely to generate strong response rates.

The frequency with which quantitative data are used in higher education makes this knowledge set essential for all who participate in institutional assessment efforts; basic quantitative skills are important elements of professional development and training programs designed to build the capacity of educators and administrators to conduct assessment processes. More advanced skills are of course necessary for those who lead the development, implementation and analysis of quantitative assessments (Pike, 2002).

Qualitative Assessment

In conducting qualitative assessment, it is important first to locate a tradition, or community, of inquiry that creates a framework for the purpose, method, and findings of desired assessment practice (Denzin & Lincoln, 2003a; Stauss & Corbin, 1998). Choosing among the five major traditions (Creswell, 1998; Denzin & Lincoln, 2003) requires assessment scholar–practitioners to think through the purpose of and rationale for the particular type of assessment that will best meet the needs and intentions of assessment planning in each specific instance. For example, assessment can be used to better understand attitudes of students toward civic engagement, to elucidate the impact of a cultural immersion experience, or to gather data about what skills students develop as the result of their participation in a resume-writing workshop. Defining and affirming the "why" of each assessment activity provides rich opportunities for determining the most appropriate qualitative approach and method (Schwandt, 2003). In each of the three examples just given, qualitative approaches will produce thick, rich results not possible through post-event forced-choice surveys (Vidich & Lyman, 2003).

The Five Traditions of Qualitative Inquiry

The five traditions of qualitative inquiry have emerged because of the recognition that the focus of a particular project or study can determine the choice of a tradition that, when used appropriately, will result in the most useful data. While assessment scholar–practitioners need not be experts in qualitative inquiry, it is consistent with national standards (i.e., those of the Council for the Advancement of Standards in Higher Educaiton, or CAS[1]) that all educators, including student affairs professionals, work from a sound theoretical base. Just as student affairs professionals weave human development theory into their work, so too should they choose qualitative assessment strategies that are grounded in theory and thus, defensible.

The five traditions are:

1. **Biography:** Biography (usually, autobiography—information recorded or otherwise offered by students themselves about themselves, or about their own experiences) provides an opportunity to increase one's understanding of students' lives and learning. By asking students to describe their perceptions of an event, interviewers can develop a detailed narrative of that student's experience (a specific autobiography). Biography can be useful when trying to document what knowledge or intrapersonal lessons students have encountered while engaged in a cultural immersion program, a study abroad, or an alternative spring break. The primary method of data gathering in a biographical approach is interviewing; among qualitative methods, this one is potentially quite resource-intensive. If biography is to be used as the means of assessing, for example, community service experiences in which a large number of students participate, it will be necessary for a number of interviewers to be prepared and available to

---

1   More information about CAS and the CAS standards is available by visiting www.cas.edu.

interview all of those students in a consistent, reproducible manner. And if documentation of learning outcomes is expected from those interviews, the interviewers must have a rubric to guide their assessment of students' changed knowledge, attitudes, or values.

2. **Phenomenology:** Phenomenology also uses interview as its primary mode of data gathering, but in contrast to biography, phenomenology seeks to understand the "Aha!" that students gain through a learning experience. Phenomenology is useful when striving to ascertain themes present in a learning experience. Like biography, it is resource-intensive, since it requires individual engagement with each student who participates in the learning experience.

3. **Grounded theory:** Grounded theory is useful for understanding what basic tenets or constructs are present in the experiences of students who participate in student programming. Grounded theory strives to bring clarity to the overall foundation of a set of experiences. For example, as a vice president seeks to understand her division's educational identity or philosophy, she may charge a colleague with the task of interviewing students to discover how they describe the purpose of student affairs. Through analyzing those interviews, themes will appear that inform the staff about students' understandings and conceptualizations of student affairs at their institution. Grounded theory can be a rich tool for discovering and guiding divisional identity. While it requires significant investments of time in interviewing or reading responses to questions from each participant, the total number of participants may be much lower than in biography; grounded theory allows for sampling (see discussion on rigor in Chapter 3), rather than interviewing every student.

4. **Ethnography:** Ethnography allows assessment scholar–practitioners to better understand how varying demographic, social, or cultural groups of students experience campus life in general, a specific set of programs, or the work and services of a department. While interviews are often the centerpiece of ethnographic inquiry, this approach allows assessment scholar–practitioners to review journals, drawings, presentations, cultural events, and other "artifacts" important to the student group being assessed. For example, in an effort to better understand how women who belong to sororities develop decision-making skills, assessment staff may interview those women and review the policies, rituals, open mottos, and other artifacts that represent important values to each sorority. Through

data gathering and analysis, assessment staff can gain greater appreciation for, empathy with, and understanding of how decisions are made within an important cultural component of campus life. Ethnography has been especially important in promoting a deeper understanding of practices, values, and behaviors in various social and cultural groups of students. Depending on the scope of inquiry, ethnography may also be quite resource-intensive to accomplish.

5. **Case study:** Case study allows assessment staff to better understand the impact of an event—the "case." Student affairs leaders or faculty members may want to gain greater knowledge and understanding of how a summer reading assignment, a first-year experience, an admissions guide program, or new student orientation influences students' acquisition of certain campus values. Through interviews, journal reviews, or blogs, assessment staff can develop clarity in their understanding of the degree to which a prescribed event or activity accomplished its intended goals. As with ethnography, the intensity of effort required for case study depends on the scope and breadth of the inquiry; case study always requires a very rich, or "thick," description of the event being reviewed.

The Application of Qualitative Approaches in Student Affairs

Self-Assessment

CAS pioneered the systematic development and deployment of professional standards and self-assessment processes and tools in higher education. Self-assessment using the CAS standards has become a routine component of internal reflection and evaluation, and is often used in preparation for external reviews, leadership transitions, and reaccreditation. The value of self-assessment in stimulating individual and departmental reconsideration and supporting continuous improvement is well known. There are, however, multiple domains of organizational function and operations; while many are covered by the CAS standards and the associated Frameworks for Assessment of Learning and Developmental Outcomes (FALDOS), others, including objective assessment of partnership and collaborative relationships, evaluation of programs and services by student users, strategic analysis, and opportunities for future advancement and program designs are not. A comprehensive self-assessment builds upon the principles that frame the CAS standards and broadens the application of self-assessment to produce integrated data that can inform institutional decision-making.

Complex Self-Assessment to Inform Organizational Decision-Making

Here we use decision-making about organizational structure as an illustration of the use of complex self-assessment methods to guide institutional policy. In many instances, a reorganization or restructuring of programs and services in academic or student affairs implemented to enhance institutional effectiveness and improve student outcomes is informed primarily by comparative institutional research and the ideas and experience of institutional leaders and consultants. Those methods are important sources of external validity; using them helps prevent restructuring in ways that simply recapitulate existing institutional idiosyncrasies and ensures that plans for a renewed structure respond to current knowledge and best practices—but in depending on external validity, institutions may overlook the ideas, expertise, and potential contributions of their own staff members. The scale, intensity, and speed of restructuring are generally determinants of the level of change resistance encountered in the process; the greater the degree of change, the more departments it involves, and the more staff members affected, the higher the chance of significant resistance. Engaging staff in a detailed self-assessment process can 1) ensure that their ideas and experience are thoughtfully gathered and considered in the overall assessment and decision-making processes, and 2) generate greater acceptance of, and more flexible attitudes toward, institutional change. To achieve those goals, the self-assessment process must emerge from asset-based assumptions (i.e., institutional staff may have helpful ideas and are important contributors to thinking about restructuring), be implemented equitably and consistently across all departments, and incorporate a balance of challenge and support.

Every divisional restructuring should be fundamentally based in mission and theory; no restructuring will have cogency and credibility absent a philosophical basis and an assessment-driven design. The following are essential elements of a recommended restructuring process based in sound self-assessment:

- Extensive qualitative and quantitative data collection through document review (annual or other regular reports, budgets, planning documents, organization charts, personnel lists), facility tours, and multiple individual and group interviews and meetings, including not only staff and faculty members and administrators, but also selected leaders of student government and student organizations.

- A consistent and carefully designed theory-based self-assessment process through which departments not only report existing operational and assessment data, but also engage their own staff, representatives of other departments inside and external to the division, and groups of students to provide critical narratives; through this process itself, as well as its results, department leaders can synthesize nuanced and textured descriptions of their present and future capacity and potential.

- A collaborative close reading, review, and analysis of each of the self-assessment submissions provided by departments in the context of the qualitative data collected earlier.

- Development of a conceptual framework for understanding and planning a new structure for the division that will best address students' needs, respond to institutional intentions to strengthen the student experience, promote greater student engagement, and foster desired student outcomes.

- Formulation and review of recommendations for a revised divisional structure, based in a sound theoretical context, that will address the institution's goals in the context of its mission, vision, and values.

Mixed Assessment Methods

Just as researchers should not select a method before determining the assessment question, higher education professionals should avoid choosing a qualitative or quantitative tactic before they have clearly discerned the characteristics of the situation, occurrence, or problem being examined and specified the purposes, stance, and intended use of the assessment. Clarity in the determination of a method derives from and provides evidence of thoughtful inquiry, which is, in itself, a strong and desirable hallmark of assessment practice.

Since assessment of learning outcomes focuses on reported human experience, a multitude of questions may be asked: What is the overarching goal of the learning experience—the domain or domains of learning to be addressed in the experience? What skill, competency, or new way of seeing the world should be the result of the learning experience? Who is the intended learner? What strategy or set of strategies provides the learning opportunity—that is, what is the vehicle for learning? What are the criteria for successful accomplishment of learning? How much learning is enough? What tools will be used to gauge and document learning? Responses to these questions create the lattice upon which assessment planning can grow. But this lattice is inevitably multimodal. It offers opportunities for both quantitative and qualitative responses, methods, and results. Higher education professionals often want to know "How much?" but we also need to understand "Who?" "Under what circumstances?" and "Through what means?"

Responses to these questions are quite specific to each institution, and they illuminate why institutions can adhere to principles of assessment practice but must avoid rigid templates. While all institutions of higher education share common features, like organizational structures, common processes, and similar arrangements of resources, colleges and universities are by in large, heterogeneous. Assessment practice embraces standard principles based on features and concerns common to higher education, but community colleges, faith-based institutions, public colleges and universities, liberal arts colleges, research universities and for-profit institutions must each engage principles of practice in ways that complement their unique identities and purposes. Table 6 illustrates this heterogeneity.

Table 6. **Examples of assessment heterogeneity across types of institutions.**

	Four-year Colleges & Universities	**Community Colleges**	**Virtual Institutions**
Who?	All graduating seniors who complete internships.	All first time college students.	Adult learners who hold degrees and are now seeking credit-bearing continuing education.
Under what circumstances?	After completing a 3-session orientation program that provides basic skills education pertinent to the approved internship.	After completing new student orientation and working with an advisor to choose and register for classes.	Upon completion of prior learning assessment that documents learners' post-degree achievements pertinent to the choice of continuing education program.
Through what means?	Pre, mid-point, and post brief individual interviews with preceptors.	Mid-term reflection essays that ask each student to describe the link between program choice and accomplishment of personal goals.	Faculty mentors' review and response to learners' self-reported acquisition of ideas and knowledge as gathered via Web-based discussion assignment.

The applied, or real world, nature of assessment practice is fraught with the inevitable ambiguities and messiness that come with investigations conducted in social settings. Often, therefore, a pragmatic response to the challenges of assessment is to adopt a mixed set of assessment methods. The evolution of research and scholarship in mixed methods techniques, practices and inquiry designs has significantly strengthened the guidance available to assessment practitioners as to what, how, and when to combine different methodologies in their practice (Tashakkori & Teddlie, 2003). Mixed methods is an important advance in responding to the varied information needs and perceptions about what constitutes valid inquiry from assessment stakeholders, but it must be engaged with careful attention to method (Teddlie & Tashakkori, 2003).

Mixed methods assessment practice is often driven by a pragmatic view, but the use of mixed methods should not be aparadigmatic—that is, the mixing of methods should not be done without consideration to the purpose, nature, and approach used in selecting and integrating methods (Greene & Caracelli, 2003; Johnson & Onwuegbuzie, 2004). A starting point for the use of mixed methods is the consideration of the underlying purpose of mixing methods. Toward this goal, Greene, Caracelli & Graham (1989) offer a starting typology in suggesting five broad categories of mixed method inquiry:

1. *Triangulation*, where multiple methods are used to find areas of convergence of data from different methods, with an aim of overcoming the biases or limitations of data gathered from any one particular method.

2. *Complementarity* seeks to use data from multiple methods to build upon each other by clarifying, enhancing, or illuminating findings between or among methods.

3. A *development* approach attempts to use data from one method to inform the implementation of another method of data gathering, as in using quantitative survey data to inform the nature and type of questions (and even the method) used in qualitative interviews or focus groups.

4. *Initiation* is an approach to mixed method inquiry that seeks to find areas of divergence or tension between methods as a means to reconsider the results of one method or the relationship of those results to a given question.

5. *Expansion* is a view of mixing methods that uses multiple methods to increase the scope, number of questions, and type of questions that an assessment project can embrace.

Assessment practitioners should understand that the use of multiple methods in a study should be done with respect for each method being employed. A critique of the pragmatic use of mixed methods that is well articulated is the *incompatibility thesis*, which asserts that because there are different underlying assumptions related to the nature of inquiry itself, different methods cannot be mixed in the same study (Greene & Caracelli, 2003; Rocco et. al., 2003). The use of multiple or mixed methods in an assessment study can be seen as an eclectic or pragmatic approach rather than an acceptance of the purist positions associated with the incompatibility thesis; the legitimacy of that approach demands at least rigor in the application of each method being used.

Once a mixed methods approach has been selected as the best process in response to the context and questions engaged in an assessment project, it is important to consider the following points (Creswell et al., 2003).

1. *Timing and sequencing* of the implementation of different methods in a study refers to when data are gathered and when methods are mixed together. Data can be gathered in parallel (at the same time), or in a sequence (one method of data gathering is completed prior to beginning another). Mixing of data can happen as a component of data gathering, as when methods are implemented in an intentional sequence, or may occur as a component of the data analysis and reporting phase.

2. *Emphasis* refers to which method is valued more than another (Creswell, 2004). It is most likely that studies will emphasize one method over another, as in a study that is primarily quantitative in nature, but also uses qualitative information to support the quantitative, or visa versa. Alternatively, a study can strive to value each method equally. Additional complexity in emphasis is inherent in considering emphasis and sequencing simultaneously; emphasis may vary with the sequencing of the study.

3. *Allocation of resources* is one of the limitations of mixing methods. The use of multiple data collection and related analysis strategies requires significant time, planning, and human capacity. Finite resources for any given study may mean that the use of mixed methods in an assessment effort will jeopardize the quality, or rigor, of the implementation of any one method. Attending to the allocation of resources in a mixed method study is essential to achieving strong implementation.

4. *Attention to mixing in analysis and reporting* ensures that a study which has gathered data using different methodologies is truly a mixed

method study, and not a collection of individual method studies. A frequent challenge in mixing methods occurs at the actual point of mixing different methods to make something new out of the results. Studies that simply report results by method seem superficially to be mixed, but miss the opportunity to address the underlying purpose and potential benefits of truly mixing methods together. Assessment practitioners must be intentional in choosing to mix methods by planning for, carefully implementing, and then reporting their data gathering activities in an integrated way; clarity about the purposes, stance, and intended use of the assessment data is a major step in ensuring the translation of those intentions into effective assessment practice.

Summary

Mixing methods is an important skill set that facilitates the ability of assessment practice to respond to varied contexts and information demands by higher education stakeholders. Crafting a multimodal lattice for assessment allows for a complex and elucidating set of interrelated data to emerge. These complex data tell a vivid story of learners, learning opportunities, and meaning-making. Designing multimodal assessment plans allows scholar–practitioners to fully blend their creativity with academic rigor. Creativity should emerge from a high-level understanding of learners, the institution's mission, its resources, and campus and community talents and expectations. While creativity brings these intangibles to life through the creation of descriptive constructs, pursuing academic rigor brings a necessary tautness to the assessment framework. For that reason, each method of assessment must be in compliance with its respective approach and, individually and together, the interwoven methods must have integrity.

CHAPTER FIVE

Capacity-Building for Assessment Practice

Bringing educators, administrators, and other professional staff together to engage in meaningful assessment requires strong leadership, clear vision, and a deep understanding of the purposes, pathways, and processes of assessment. Determining the readiness and competency of faculty and staff to fully engage in each step of the assessment process is an integral component. Devoting sufficient key resources—especially time, focus, funds, and leadership commitment—to build strong professional capacity is an essential institutional investment that ensures all participants are prepared and fully capable of engaging in each step of the assessment process. *Educators will not learn to do effective assessment simply by reading a book or manual; capacity-building requires curricular, experiential learning with robust opportunities for practice and feedback.*

Four Primary Areas of Competency

An understanding of how, where, when, and why intentional learning occurs at every level and in every element of the institution is essential to the development and implementation of assessment of student learning outcomes. The capacity to develop, implement, assess, and report student learning outcomes embraces four main areas of competency:

1. **Mapping** learning

2. **Integrating** learning

3. **Supporting** students as learners

4. **Assessing** the outcomes of learning

Fundamental to each and any of the four is knowledge of current concepts of learning itself. Competency in all four areas will enable educators to do more than simply write learning outcome statements in a rote manner from templates or guidelines; well-prepared educators will use the process of writing and assessing learning outcomes to guide the development, improvement, and coordination of both academic and out-of-classroom or experiential learning programs. Competency among educators permits assessment to have, and fulfill, its purpose; insufficient preparation turns assessment into an empty exercise.

Mapping Learning

Mapping learning requires educators to consider all places—virtual and geographic—of learning in students' lives during their time of enrollment in college. Questions like these facilitate the development of a rich conceptual map of student learning on campus: "Where do students indigenously learn?" "To what extent do our intentional learning activities, including programs or courses of study, locate themselves in those places?" "How do students use technology (including course software, social networking Web sites [such as MySpace and Facebook], Web searches, and digital libraries) to communicate, mentor one another, find and qualify information, and learn?" and "How can the institution work in harmony with students' current modes of learning?" Responses to these and similar questions begin to generate a *topography* of learning that reveals opportunities and challenges; the mapping process identifies areas in which intentional learning related to institutional goals does or does not occur and places in which certain erratic, random, or unintentional learning experiences that have substantial value can be made intentional and routine. The fact that learning (and assessment) begins informally does not mean they cannot become intentional.

Addressing learning topographically infers not only that learning happens multi-centrically, inside and outside the classroom (and in both "real" and virtual spaces), but also that understanding and supporting learning require interdisciplinary, integrative lenses and perspectives (Keeling, 2004; Keeling, 2006). To map learning is also to affirm the possibility of surprise—discovering that learning does, or does not, happen when, and where, and how it was expected (for example: students may learn—meaning gather information, request clarification, consider options and behaviors, and commit to a plan, not just "play"—through their use of social networking Web sites; indeed, distinguishing "learning" from "play" becomes more difficult—and perhaps less relevant—in a globally networked, digital world in which computer games, social networking sites, and chat rooms become learning tools). Just as institutional planners learn where to put sidewalks by observing pathways marked by people's walking patterns, educators may learn where to place or emphasize learning experiences by documenting the places in which learning naturally occurs.

Mapping learning teaches the contours, relationships, pathways, and distances of learning itself, and what comes to be known about learning, and how and where it happens, can influence institutional policy and strategy for supporting student achievement. Mapping learning is, therefore, itself a process of assessment (i.e., the locations in which learning happens are observed and documented) that requires the rigor, commitment, and expertise essential in all assessment practices. It is not enough to *think we know* how and where students learn; asking diligently and frequently to ensure that we have current, complete, and nuanced answers that are relevant and meaningful across the diversity of our students is a commitment that will support greater institutional effectiveness.

Integrating Learning

Integrating learning includes conceptualizing and developing learning opportunities that tighten the intellectual and social fabric woven by students' interactions with the institution's entire catalogue of learning experiences. Students' successive encounters with learning activities, which are primarily vertically organized (disciplines, departments, majors, courses, discussion sections, labs; leadership development, diversity, counseling), can seem disconnected, unrelated, and lacking synthesis and meaning, absent the influence and mediation of some institutionally sponsored horizontal, or integrative, structure. Institutions can intentionally support and co-create such horizontal structures (such as first-year transition programs, lower division advising, and service learning experiences) to give coherence to students' learning experiences, increase their capacity to make meaning across disciplines and courses, and support student achievement (Keeling, Underhile, & Wall, 2007).

Some very capable, well-prepared, and high-functioning students can accomplish such integration independently—but for many others, the sequence of general education courses, major requirements, and electives may have little internal cohesion and no sense of conceptual linkages; what is learned in one place, or course, may not be infused into learning in other contexts. Integrating learning—which is actualized by purposively designing and weaving this fabric of "horizontal" transformative experiences—can increase coherence between and among for-credit and not-for-credit learning activities; foster the development of a student body that collectively understands and supports the mission of the institution; generate a synthesis of institutional data sets that provides a more robust and multidimensional understanding of student experience; and produce a complex, yet clear, assessment portfolio.

The work of integrating learning occurs primarily at the level of institutional policy, curriculum, and structure and requires the diligent collaboration of faculty, academic leaders, administrators, and student affairs professionals. Developing renewed transition experiences for first-time-in-college freshmen, transfer students, and graduating seniors that create conceptual and practical bridges between phases of students' lives is a strong example; success requires the participation of educators in several disciplines (including student affairs) and results in the creation of a broad new cross-institutional strategy (transition programs provided for entering students regardless of intended major or academic pathway; clustered intentional learning experiences for students preparing for the world of work and citizenship).

Supporting Students as Learners

Supporting students as learners requires not just offering specific cognitive strategies and remedial programs and services, but also the application of policy and strategy to routine institutional operations in both academic programs and student life activities. Applying the policies and strategies derived from attempts to integrate learning in academic and student affairs programs might involve coupling more tightly the active and reflective elements of learning experiences (requiring, for example, that students who participate in service learning projects in the community complete journals or discuss their observations and describe what they learned in structured conversations with program directors or advisors), closely linking classroom and out-of-classroom learning activities (ensuring that undergraduate internships have specific learning goals coordinated with the content and syllabi of students' courses), and bridging cognitive and experiential learning opportunities (developing ways to debrief students who attend meetings of government or not-for-profit entities to see local representative government in action). The effect of these couplings, or linkages, is to increase the perceived coherence of the whole educational experience; students begin to see the relationships between what they are learning in one context and their activities in many others. Further, students have additional opportunities to make meaning through watching their peers engage in these coherent learning experiences.

Neither student affairs educators nor members of the academic faculty can accomplish such integrations of learning activities alone; supporting student learning across the college experience is of necessity interdisciplinary, cross-functional, and collaborative. Supporting student learning is inherently horizontal, rather than vertical, in the geometry of institutions. Both the process of integrating learning—which, as described earlier, has a macroscopic, structural, policy driven quality—and that of supporting students as learners through the deployment of various activities that link and maximize learning experiences—which has a more tailored, individualized focus—are necessary and essential partners in making the institution effective in promoting student learning. Together, integrating and supporting learning simultaneously add depth and breadth to the institution and its learning opportunities.

Assessing the Outcomes of Learning

Assessing the outcomes of learning requires competency in the development, implementation, measurement, and reporting of the achievement of student learning outcomes (see a discussion of the nature and structure of student learning outcomes in Chapter 2; Chapter 4 provides an overview of the use of both qualitative and quantitative techniques of assessment of learning outcomes). Competency in documenting the impact of learning is developed through an intentional and curricular process of professional capacity-building that can be neither instantaneous nor glib. That process requires:

- Needs assessments (to determine the "starting point" in terms of faculty and staff knowledge, skills, and attitudes).

- The acquisition and application of new knowledge and skills (e.g., how to write an assessment plan that produces useful data, understanding descriptive and inferential statistics, or knowing how and when to use a rubric in doing qualitative inquiry).

- Learning and applying a new vocabulary and rhetoric (about various assessment methods, for example—pre- and post-surveys vs. structured interviews, journaling, or direct observation).

- Development of an authentically collaborative work style (since student learning occurs, and must be assessed, across campus, not simply within disciplines, individual departments, or divisions).

- Comfort with getting and receiving constructive feedback (a positive consequence of collaboration).

- Maturation of positive attitudes toward and facility in understanding data acquisition, analysis, and reporting through qualitative, quantitative, and mixed methods (see Chapter 4).

- The exercise of professional resiliency (things do not always go well the first time out).

- Formulation of a strong commitment to the results-oriented, data-driven improvement of programs, services, transactions, and activities—as noted many times in this monograph, assessment should never be done just for assessment's sake.

Learning to Document Learning

Learning how to document learning is not a mechanical process of applying some template or workbook to myriad activities and programs; it is a professional re-commitment to a different way of thinking about, doing, and assessing the work. Institutions fail at the assessment of learning when they trivialize the effort, underestimate the significance of the shift in perspective that is required, simply expect educators (whether faculty members or student affairs professionals) to add it as one more separate piece of their work requirements, or balk at providing the professional development curriculum and resources that it demands.

To achieve essential competencies in mapping, integrating, supporting, and assessing student learning, educators must be able to:

- Explain the roles of assessment in 1) demonstrating accountability, 2) creating integrative, horizontal structures to support student success, 3) supporting transformative learning, and 4) defining the topography of learning across the institution.

Discuss the concepts of methods, stance, use, and values in assessment; explain how the intended use of assessment results is related to the design of assessment processes and the selection of methods.

Explain how student learning outcomes are developed—not by trying to attach some statement of learning to existing programs and activities, but by first determining what overall learning goals are needed to accomplish the mission of the institution; then deciding what programs, activities, or learning experiences will provide achievement that satisfies those goals; then selecting specific components of the overall learning goals that will be addressed in each program or activity; and, finally, defining specific student learning outcomes pertinent to each of those program- or activity-based learning goals.

Describe and explain the essential roles of developing, implementing, assessing, and documenting student learning outcomes; differentiate student learning outcomes from indicators of operational effectiveness, student satisfaction, or efficiency; and explain how the concept of institutional effectiveness is linked to students' achievement of desired learning outcomes.

Explain and illustrate the key elements of the creation of effective, measurable, and meaningful student learning outcomes linked to assessment plans that generate useful, reliable, and credible data; be able to describe and teach those elements to colleagues and peers.

Describe the core features of cogent and effective assessment plans, methods, and processes with which to evaluate the achievement of desired student learning outcomes; explain how various assessment methods are best matched with various purposes and outcomes; discuss the application of qualitative, quantitative, and mixed methods to different kinds of assessment inquiries.

Explain linkages among the institution's mission, strategic plan, and student learning outcomes at institutional, divisional, departmental, and programmatic levels.

 Describe cross-departmental, inter-divisional, and interdisciplinary processes for linking the assessment of student learning outcomes to quality improvement, program evaluation, and resource allocation.

As the previous sections suggest, building capacity to assess student learning outcomes is a complex, demanding process; it requires four domains of competency that are linked through multiple intersecting learning goals. Graduate programs that prepare disciplinary faculty or student affairs professionals have begun to address those competencies through their curricula—but many practitioners, scholars, and teachers now serving in colleges and universities of all types have not had sufficient preparation to undertake the work of assessing student learning in a serious, productive way. Just filling out forms and templates or mechanically following the step-by-step instructions in workbooks will not produce skilled assessments; one professional development workshop, no matter how capable the presenter(s) or how good the handouts, will not produce sustainable competency or support the development of a culture of evidence and assessment. A different—and more comprehensive—approach is necessary.

A Curricular Approach to Capacity-Building

What is needed, instead, is true institutional investment in capacity-building through ongoing professional development and training. This professional development must be long-term, curricular, iterative, and inspiring. As is true in any other curriculum, the elements, or components, must make sense in and of themselves and in relation to one another; taken together, they should have coherence and meaning. Each component builds upon the last; participants gain knowledge and skills sequentially, integrating new material or resources with what has been learned before. Having learned about assessment (including its purposes, stance, methods, use, and values) and its role in supporting student learning and success, participants should then sequentially acquire the ability to:

 Distinguish student learning outcomes from operational indicators and metrics, including measures of student satisfaction.

 Define a student learning outcome.

 Explain overall institutional student learning outcomes and their relationship to mission.

Describe specific intentional learning experiences that the institution provides to address those overall outcomes; identify the geographic, curricular, and/or digital locations of those experiences.

Discuss how specific programs, services, and learning experiences provide support for students' achievement of desired institutional learning outcomes.

Derive and use, in collaboration with colleagues, a common format and structure for writing student learning outcomes.

Design robust assessment plans to address measurement of the achievement of learning outcomes.

Differentiate various methods of assessment (qualitative, quantitative, and mixed methods, and categories, or communities of practice, within each).

Select an assessment method that fits the needs of each intended learning outcome.

Write an assessment plan that incorporates sufficient detail—with enough clarity—to be understood by others.

Implement the process of assessment of selected student learning outcomes.

Collect accurate, reliable, and trustworthy data of the type required by the assessment plan.

Analyze both qualitative and quantitative data logically and effectively.

Report results clearly and transparently.

Explain how results and their implications can be transformed into information to guide program improvement.

Understand what roles institutional politics should, and should not, play in assessment processes.

Summary

Institutional officers and administrators should expect that the whole process of building staff capacity and expertise for assessment of student learning outcomes will require one to three years of professional development experiences (depending on the frequency and intensity of those activities) supported by appropriate digital and print resources (Piper, 2007). This does not mean that the first student learning outcomes are not assessed for a year or more—carefully planned and implemented professional development curricula will produce learning outcome data within six to twelve months. But capacity must, and will, deepen over time; the quality of outcomes defined, data collected, reports issued, and improvements enacted will increase over years. And, as a component of institutional accountability, the assessment of student learning outcomes will inevitably flex and adjust with the political, academic, and social context of the institution; professional development is, therefore, not finite and must remain adaptive.

CHAPTER SIX

Assessment in Practice

I n Chapter 2, we discussed the importance of basing assessment practice in theory; here, we extend that discussion, deriving a conceptual map of assessment in practice in higher education. Principles of community organization can be effectively and usefully applied to the process of determining the most effective strategies for introducing, implementing, sustaining, and refining assessment practice in a department, division, or whole institution. Concepts adapted from attitude and behavior change theories and diffusion of innovation theory can elucidate how new information and practices get shared and adopted or map how true collaboration can be generated and brought to fruition. Public school districts at both elementary and secondary levels have historically sought and utilized strategies to coordinate school health and student learning (Fetro, 1998). Work in all of these arenas is exceedingly useful to scholar–practitioners in higher education as they map assessment in practice.

A Conceptual Map of Assessment in Practice

Applying Concepts of Community Organization to Assessment in Higher Education

Community organization practice is a rich blend of psychology, education, sociology, and anthropology; it rests on the acquisition and synthesis of data about the functioning of people, structures, and systems in communities, and it supports an assessment of the flexibility, velocity, adaptability, and capacity of the community as a whole, as well as its constituent groups. Because assessment practice has both *organizational reflection* and *institutional change* at its core, a strong understanding of how campuses, as communities of learning, respond to stimuli for change is a necessary and vital component of assessment planning and practice. Examples in Chapter 2 offered a useful review of three types of community organization; as Chapter 5 shows, building staff readiness and capacity to engage in assessment practice requires strong leadership, clarity of purpose, and a balanced, ongoing program of professional development. While some colleagues have exemplary knowledge of and skill in assessment planning, others will find the opportunity overwhelming, frustrating, and taxing.

Addressing the concerns and educational needs of all colleagues requires thoughtful and transparent planning. A common barrier to authentic and successful capacity-building is ineffective leadership, especially at the departmental level, that gives into the change resistance of staff members (and even managers)—the most common manifestation of which is, "I don't have time to do it." A leader who cannot mobilize and inspire staff to begin and sustain assessment activities may end up completing all of the assessment work in an effort to squelch staff anxiety and avoid conflict. No institution, nor any component of one, can build the capacity of staff if leaders hoard, or refuse to insist on sharing, the hard work. In community organization practice this challenge is often described in terms of power struggles, role delineation, and resistance to change. While cumbersome, the appearance and resolution of these elements of organizational functioning can indicate the emergence of healthy organizations.

Nurturing Change

Attitude and behavior change theories and diffusion theories can also shed light on how change can best be nurtured. Roger's diffusion of innovation theory, described and applied in Chapter 2, also includes descriptions of the characteristics of different types of individuals and how those individuals with various combinations of those characteristics respond to change (Rogers, 1995). Higher education professionals often discuss stages of change as a theory, but less often do discussions of how to promote change in practical terms occur. Further investigation of attitude and behavior change theories can provide much needed guidance in determining how and to whom to disseminate information and examples; skill development opportunities; persuasive communication; or positive reinforcement through constructive criticism and informative praise. Understanding and responding to the unique needs of each group of faculty and staff is in and of itself a component of developing and sustaining sound assessment practice; at the same time, defining and documenting those needs should not be allowed unnecessarily to delay the establishment of high expectations for increasing the capacity of all educators to do excellent assessment work. Complaints that amount to "But I don't know how!" may represent authentic needs assessment data—but they can also be manifestations of change resistance.

Just as we seek to develop learning outcomes that are developmentally appropriate for students, so too we must consider the developmental aspects of our own professional preparation. To a great extent, this consideration sheds light on how the diversity of higher education professionals can work across disciplines and areas of expertise—while some colleagues have great knowledge of program planning, others have expertise in qualitative or quantitative data methods, and still others in student development theory. Linking internal intellectual resources to one another results in a stronger overall institutional identity (which begets and can sustain a true horizontality of practice).

A Practical Model for Assessment Planning

Integrating concepts and ideas from community organization, change and diffusion theories, and school health practice supports the development of a practical model for assessment planning and practice, as depicted in Table 7. Assessment planning is a complex activity. While it is not necessarily difficult, it is intensive, and it addresses a dynamic set of interrelated activities, each of which has different phases—so it can be useful to plan assessment in stages.

Table 7. **A practical model for assessment planning.**

Stages of Assessment Planning	Steps for Assessment Planning
Stage 1 This may include steps 1-3 listed to the right. During this stage, a foundation is established that anchors and provides ballast to future assessment activities.	1. Determine who within the institution, division, or department will take leadership of assessment activities; clearly communicate the dimensions of that person's leadership role and expectations. This role is often defined as that of an "assessment champion." 2. Consider the talents, aptitudes, and areas of expertise present among colleagues and establish an assessment team to work closely with the leader and also with other faculty or staff. 3. Develop an internal capacity-building strategy that provides staff and faculty with accurate information, introduces them to key concepts of student learning, student development, and assessment practice; decide what elements of this strategy will be addressed by formal, intentional professional development and training, and what components will require either hands-on practice within the structure of existing positions and roles or self-study.

Stages of Assessment Planning	Steps for Assessment Planning
Stage 2 During this stage, which includes steps 4 and 5, an infrastructure emerges. The creation of a glossary will result in a common language. But more importantly, the process of developing the glossary allows time and resources to be devoted to asking important questions, engaging in discourse that brings clarity and rationale to assessment activities. Step 5 brings common concerns to the table and should include candid conversations about perceptions and realities of who on campus "owns" assessment; how assessment differs from institutional research; the roles of faculty, staff, and administrators, and their respective strengths and weaknesses.	4. Create a glossary of terms that brings clarity and common understanding to pertinent concepts; make that glossary easily accessible. It is more important to have consistency within the institution than to make the institution's terms exactly the same as those of some other institution or professional organization.
	5. Consider and respond to potential barriers, impediments, and challenges, including power dynamics, internal departmental or institutional politics, and various manifestations of change resistance.
Stage 3 This stage includes the next three steps, 6 through 8, which are the processes of inquiry and assessment with which to inform the assessment plan. Important questions to ask during this stage include: Where do students naturally learn on our campus and in our community? What are the sociographics of our students? What is important to them? How do they learn? Why did they choose our institution? How can we best serve and educate them? What programs, student organizations, professional honoraries, and services are already in place to promote student learning and development? What programs and services could be enhanced? With what members of the faculty and staff should we develop partnerships?	6. Map existing campus and community resources—an institutional topography of learning.
	7. Determine learning and developmental needs of students in relation to the institution's overall desired student learning outcomes.
	8. Determine program strengths and areas for improvement—that is, define what programs address what areas of students' learning and developmental needs, and then study the effectiveness of each of those programs in addressing those needs.

Stages of Assessment Planning	Steps for Assessment Planning
Stage 4 This stage incorporates the final two steps, 9 and 10, which synthesize much of the information gathered in the previous steps. Data about program and personnel talent can be arranged in a matrix that illustrates program names, departmental objectives, leadership, and professional development needs. In some ways this stage is the culmination of all the planning. And at this point the stage is set for developing and assessing student learning outcomes.	9. Develop an assessment curriculum, including a scope and sequence that describes and illustrates who will lead what program, what the learning outcomes are for each program, when and how learning will be assessed, and when and how data will be gathered, analyzed, and disseminated.
	10. Based on sound assessment data, evaluate the quality, or effectiveness, of programs and institute processes of sustainability or improvement.

Elements of Assessment Practice

Designing Student Learning Outcomes

Designing student learning outcomes is an iterative process; we address the basic requirements of student learning outcomes in previous chapters. As much art as science, developing student learning outcomes is a non-linear, yet step-by-step process. Basic questions to ask include:

- What group(s) of students
- Who participate in
- What activity, course, program, or service
- Will be able to do, know, or value what
- At what frequency or level of accomplishment
- As determined by what means

This set of questions can serve as a template for beginning to bring unity in how the assessment team and other colleagues begin to understand, think about, and describe the process of crafting student learning outcomes.

Selecting Methods of Assessment

A common impediment to assessment is difficulty determining the mode or method of assessment. From a very practical perspective, choosing the method for assessing the extent to which the learning outcome was accomplished is dependent on resources. For a very large event like a career fair or new student orientation, resource limitations would not allow for individual interviews to be conducted with all participants; in this example, an online survey might be the best method of gathering data. In contrast, however, students who were enrolled in an alternative spring break experience that was limited to 25 participants might easily be debriefed by five well-prepared interviewers. Taking into consideration the likely number of participants in the activity or program that is to serve as the vehicle for learning and then determining the ratio of participants to staff or faculty who are assigned that particular learning outcome can act as a useful strategy for selecting the method of data gathering. See Chapter 4 for both a discussion of the relative resource-intensity of various approaches to qualitative assessment and a detailed review of qualitative, quantitative, and mixed methods.

The Assessment Calendar

Choosing the time and venue for gathering assessment data in any specific instance can be made far more manageable through the development of a thoughtful quarterly, semester, or academic-year assessment plan for a department, division, or whole institution. In doing so, it is essential to take into consideration the natural flow of academic and institutional requirements and activities that may force competition for resources, including student participation. Most institutions will want to avoid administering too many surveys to students during the same general timeframe (e.g., the months of October or February); similarly, gathering sound qualitative assessment data through methods such as biography will be more likely to succeed if not implemented during exams. After the assessment calendar is established, adequate communication strategies, such as a blog or assessment listserv, may be put in place to keep everyone informed.

Review of Assessment Activity

Monitoring the progress, impediments, and unexpected successes of assessment activities is a necessary component of assessment practice. Quality assessment practice includes organizational reflection—that activity and the sharing of lessons learned builds capacity, deepens professional understanding of the nature of student learning, and increases organizational resiliency. Resilient institutions of higher education enjoy greater transparency, professional integrity, social connectedness, and a shared sense of purpose. Engaging in a review of assessment activity does not mean, and should not be represented or taken as, monitoring staff for corrective actions, but serves as a strategy for continuously improving practice, identifying professional development and training needs, and discovering institutional identity as documented by the tight coupling of mission, practice, and outcomes.

Responding to Assessment Data

Developing strategies for responding to assessment data further increases professional integrity and ensures that change in programs is logical, coherent, and defensible. Data from the assessment of achievement of student learning outcomes, interpreted both by individual program or activity and in the aggregate, inform the extent to which intentional learning experiences (programs, courses, services, etc.) are functioning as they were planned and intended. The more closely defined student learning outcomes align with stated program objectives, the more effectively student learning and development can be assessed, guided, and supported. Discovering that programs are not functioning as they intended is not necessarily evidence that the program is "bad"; it merely indicates that the learning strategy present in the program is not well-suited to enhancing students' acquisition of knowledge, values, or abilities. While it may be very difficult for established, long-serving staff members to discover that some legacy program does not perform as intended, that knowledge is essential to program integrity and the fulfillment of institutional mission.

Reporting and Refinement of Results

Reporting the results of outcome data should happen in three stages: 1) Report to those charged with assessment, 2) Report to those who have contributed to assessment efforts—the full assessment team, and 3) Report to the campus community, including students. Prior to the third stage, however, leaders should determine action steps for program refinement. While some programs may function exactly as intended, others may need to be revised and improved, and still others may be considered for discontinuation. It is never wise to release assessment data before determining what will be done in response to those data; no leader wants to be confronted by students or others about her plans for addressing assessment results before those plans have been made.

Careful consideration should be given to the level of administrative response to any given set of assessment data. Comprehensive data accrue over time; it is wise to engage in thoughtful principles of evaluation and inquiry when using data to determine program worth. The bigger the decision that needs to be made, the more robust should be the data supporting it—which means that some decisions must await additional data collection in a subsequent semester or year. Further, careful consideration should be given to decisions about what elements of programs need what types of refinement. A very good and effective program could suffer because of poor timing, less than optimal venue, or lack of marketing. Student learning outcomes data offer myriad opportunities for administrators to view many aspects of programs. In this way, they should accompany, but also rise above, simple output measures that merely describe the number of students who participate. Just as the quality of data becomes more complex, so will the depth of thought and collaboration necessary for making changes to programs.

Summary

Conceptualizing assessment practice includes a comprehensive beginning, thoughtful implementation, and rigorous response. Student learning outcomes data are one, and perhaps the most important and necessarily rigorous component, of assessment in higher education today. However, those data should be linked to program reviews, quality improvement, studies of students' needs and satisfaction, internal and external reviews (including accreditation), and institutional strategic planning (Wright, 2002). Colleges and universities that embrace comprehensive assessment practice enjoy the benefits of internal and external credibility that stem from a fundamental organizational transparency that links mission to practice; it sends the powerful message, "This is who we are; these are the skills and competencies that we strive to instill in students; these programs and efforts are how we do that; and these data illustrate the sum of our efforts." While recent political pressures have highlighted assessment largely (or exclusively) as a tool for responding to external demands for accountability, authentic assessment, as this monograph emphasizes repeatedly, goes above and beyond that. Authentic assessment of student learning attests to each institution's will and purpose—and to its determination to serve the public good.

CHAPTER SEVEN

The Costs of Assessment in Higher Education

T he old adage, "you get what you pay for" can aptly be applied to the consideration of the costs of assessment in higher education. Those costs are not simply fiscal, but rather can be observed in the expenditure of financial, human, organizational, political, and symbolic capital. The cost of assessment activities cannot simply be accounted for on a fiscal ledger, then, but appears in a broader accounting of the associated leadership challenges of higher education. A fundamental understanding of the costs of assessment in the greater context of all of the expenditures necessary to sustain higher education rests on the basic reality that assessment is a political and symbolic activity rooted in the complex organizational dynamics of colleges and universities; the consideration of the cost of assessment is therefore not simply addressed by budgeting for assessment activities, though the financial outlays required must be considered, but demands a larger inquiry into the related costs associated with exploring the processes and outcomes of higher education.

Of course the whole cost of assessment is also very much about the dollars and time necessary to carry out the processes of inquiry. An assessment process that is under-resourced risks being incomplete, wasteful, frustrating, not illuminative, or perceived as invalid. Under-resourced assessment practices then have both financial and institutional consequences. The associated costs, which might also be understood as risks, have strong symbolic, political, and organizational overtones. Assessment activities are not inexpensive (whether measured by dollars spent or time invested), and they also require the investment of the political and organizational capital necessary to engage in a process of inquiry that gathers meaningful information. A process that has limited resources in money, time, and organizational commitment is likely to yield results that are narrow, and the report of that work will likely sit on a shelf, or never escape the confines of somebody's hard drive. On the other hand, an assessment effort to which the institution has made a significant commitment of resources in money, time, organizational priority, and high expectations has significantly more potential for being illuminative, and, therefore, useful. The examination of cost then is necessarily one of multiple facets of resource allocation to assessment activities.

The Symbolic and Political Dimensions of Cost

Understanding the symbolic and political costs associated with assessment in higher education is essential to planning for and implementing a successful assessment effort. The symbolic and political costs of assessment rest in the choices of what activities, methods, and people will be involved in a given effort. Given constrained resources for any activity in higher education, not everything can be assessed, and not all assessment efforts will be the same. This is only to say that there always will be choices made about what, how, and when assessment will be implemented in any institution of higher education, and that those choices create significant symbolic and political costs that must be understood, addressed, managed, and monitored.

The selection of what will be assessed holds particular symbolic and political importance for leaders in higher education making assessment decisions. If we choose to primarily assess graduation and retention rates, then we identify clearly what is symbolically valued, to what the institution gives its attention, and by what criteria the institution seeks to be understood and evaluated. The selection of what is measured may of course to a variable degree reflect external demands, but nonetheless provides strong symbolic clues as to how success is defined by the institution itself. An institution's choice to assess student success through measurement of gains in critical thinking, civic engagement or global/cultural understanding *in addition to* externally demanded reports about retention and graduation makes a strong symbolic statement about what is valued in that institution, and how the institution feels others should determine whether it is meeting its goals and serving the public good.

But the choice to have assessment include measures of gains in critical thinking, civic engagement, or global/cultural understanding has real symbolic, political and resource costs. Symbolically and politically, the selection of a set of learning outcomes to measure eschews other outcomes that won't be assessed; while the assessment of critical thinking may be important, so too is an appreciation for the arts, or knowledge of the fundamental content of a particular discipline. Politically speaking, should the institution choose to assess those things about which there is consensus of importance, and thus about which there is less political cost associated with assessment, or to engage in assessment of some measure or goal of learning about which there is less consensus of importance, and therefore a higher political cost?

Method selection also influences the symbolic and political costs of assessment. While there are dollar and time variations in the use of different methods of inquiry, decisions about the methodology used in assessment are fraught with symbolic and political costs. Selections of method for expediency, external validity, or practicality are not simply fiscal decisions, but choices that reflect value orientations toward different ways of knowing. Different methodological approaches can be highly contentious inside the academy (imagine the discussion at a faculty meeting about the relative value of qualitative and quantitative measures, or at a university senate session about collaboration between the faculty and student affairs educators); similarly, different methods may have lesser or greater worth as interpreted by those outside the institution. There may also be important symbolic and political costs in relationship to the type of information gathered from any particular method. So educators planning the methods to be used in assessment activities must consider more than expediency and practicality; they have to attend to the underlying issues of what types of knowledge are valued by the institution and its stakeholders.

A third dimension of the symbolic and political costs associated with assessment begins with the perception of assessment within the organization (a department, division, or whole institution). Assessment is an activity seldom associated with neutral organizational feelings; rather, the decision to plan and launch assessment practices within an organization is often met with a broad spectrum of reactions, including variations of fear, concern, and (believe it or not) even excitement, depending upon the context and circumstances. If the purpose of assessment is to strengthen and improve student learning, assessment efforts may be highly valued and received positively—assuming a sufficient case can be made that the assessment work will, in fact, improve student learning—but even routine, less ambitious assessment efforts can have real symbolic and political costs. Take the example of student ratings of professors, a common assessment effort at the end of an academic course; these routine assessments can be nonetheless symbolically threatening to many faculty members, especially those who are untenured. Institutional attempts to conduct instructor assessments, though they are frequently seen as limited, practical, and highly benign, may still generate significant dissent among faculty—so performing them incurs a real political cost.

The political and symbolic costs of assessment are key factors that make carrying out assessment a leadership challenge. The human and organizational cost of assessment is palatable when assessment is done well. To engage in inquiry about the effectiveness of learning experiences when the answer is unknown is inevitably to place individuals and organizations in a state of uncomfortable ambiguity. Among all educators, allowing one's work to be examined means opening oneself up to critique and dissonance. The process of "putting yourself out there" to have your efforts examined is disconcerting, even when conducted with the best of intent (which is not always the case). But assessment of one's program(s) is not a personnel evaluation. While we may be eager to have our favorite student program examined to determine if it is meeting our student learning objectives, it is threatening to think that it may not be, and any good process of inquiry can almost be guaranteed to produce results that are both positive and negative. Thomas Schwandt (1996) writes that good inquiry always leaves oneself open to change, whether the subject of assessment is an organization undergoing inquiry, or the inquirer as an individual. To learn something new is to initiate change, or to miss an opportunity to change.

While faculty members are often accustomed to critiques of their work from both internal and external observers through processes such as peer review of manuscripts submitted for publication, discussion of research results presented at conferences, and, of course, the promotion and tenure process itself, those processes are less familiar to student affairs educators, who may, therefore, perceive them as more threatening. On the other hand, student affairs educators may be less resistant to instituting assessment processes to detect achievement of the accomplishment of student learning outcomes, because they do not have any other system—such as grades—through which to claim that learning has been assessed.

Accounting the Costs of Assessment

The costs to individuals and organizations of assessment are, first, that the activities of assessment take time and energy, precisely the things that so few working professionals (be they students, student affairs professionals, staff, faculty or academic administrative roles) have to spare. Thus, assessment is an activity that for many is added to, rather than integrated with other activities in, their already busy lives. Participation in data gathering takes real time, whether to fill out a survey, take an exam, participate in an interview, or be a part of a focus group. Gathering, analyzing, and reporting on an assessment project demands both time and energy—and always requires assigning priority to the assessment project over other also-needed and justified demands on time and mindshare. Often the demands of conducting assessment parallel the kinds of effort needed for conducting research: i.e., significant sustained cognitive engagement, which is a process hard to fit into and between already overbooked schedules. The obvious time and energy cost concerns regarding assessment can obscure the more significant symbolic and political costs associated with opening one's work and efforts up to scrutiny.

Planning for the Costs of Assessment

The costs of assessment then, must be considered in multiple dimensions, like assessment itself. The idea of planning for meeting those costs must be seen as being complex, multi-layered, and part of the organizational context of higher education. Planning for assessment at a basic level involves first considering the probable costs in terms of dollars and time required to conduct a competent process of inquiry. There are three dimensions in planning for costs at this basic level: 1) determining and gathering appropriate human resources, 2) planning appropriate time frames for activities, and 3) developing authentic and reasonable budgets.

Human resources: The human resources requirements of various assessment efforts and projects differ; see, for example, the discussion of various levels of resource intensity for qualitative assessment methods in Chapter 4. Lee Shulman (2007) has suggested that there are different stakes and projected learning yields from different types of assessment; some projects are low stakes and low yield, while others are high stakes and high yield (still others are low stakes and low yield, or high stakes and low yield). The question of who should be engaging in what type of assessment implies (rightly) that individuals appropriately have different capacities, or competencies, to engage in assessment activities; educators with higher capacity would, appropriately, be assigned to higher stakes/higher yield assessment projects. Recognizing that different projects call upon different levels and types of expertise is, then, essential to assigning human resources for conducting assessment and is as important as determining the type of assessment in which to engage. Furthermore, efforts to assess student learning that are intended primarily to improve programmatic function, but are not intended to be externally reported, will require different levels of commitment of expertise than efforts that are a part of institutional preparation for external reporting (e.g., for accreditation, press coverage, or institutional marketing). For low stakes efforts that have strong potential for yielding good information, it is quite possible to prepare, engage, and count on staff members who have little technical expertise under the guidance of a competent inquirer (trained in assessment, evaluation, or institutional research) to complete an assessment project. On the other hand, assessment projects that have both high stakes and the potential for high learning yield (as one would hope all projects would) are likely to require the dedicated time of individuals who have specific preparation, training, and expertise. The determination of human resource needs is thus appropriately linked to the type of assessment that is planned.

Major factors to consider in determining the cost in human resources for assessment projects include:

- The type of assessment effort that is being planned. As noted earlier, projects differ from low stakes program examinations to institution-wide examination of student learning outcomes that will be reported to external entities and carefully scrutinized, with potentially important consequences to the institution.

- Existing organizational capacity to engage in assessment. Not all organizations (departments, divisions, etc.) throughout an institution are equally prepared to engage in an assessment process. Building organizational capacity to engage effectively in assessment is a key element to be considered and accounted for in projecting the cost of assessment activity (see also Chapter 5).

- The level of existing internal professional expertise in assessment, i.e., the experience and technical inquiry skills of members of the faculty and student affairs educators (more discussion in Chapters 5 and 6). Although there may be significant costs associated with professional development and training efforts, failing to prepare educators to engage effectively in assessment creates a poor administrative legacy and severely restrains the efficacy of assessment work. Given the potential symbolic and political costs of assessment, no institution can afford those consequences.

- Determination of the technical demands of a given assessment effort. Many individuals (faculty members, student affairs educators, administrators, and others) can be trained to assist in data collection (through surveys, interviews, focus groups, observations, etc.), but more specific technical preparation is often needed to design assessment processes, build tools, conduct analysis, and report on results.

In a human resources budget, the primary cost of assessment is always associated with time and expertise. Major budget elements of assessment include:

- The full-time equivalent (FTE) effort of current institutional staff members who will be engaging in assessment. This cost usually is not a new one, but rather reflects the increased, deferred, or replaced work of individuals in an organization. It is the institutional reflection of the question asked by staff members themselves: "What do I stop doing in order to do this?"

- The cost of acquiring the necessary expertise to complete a project, often reflected in the use of internal expertise, hiring of new staff members, or consultant expenses.

Time: Accurate estimates of the time necessary to carry out an assessment project are essential in cost accounting. Often the need for assessment information is immediate and, thus, time frames are compressed (sometimes in ridiculous ways), but, in general, good planning for assessment can be done with sensitivity to time constraints and always helps ensure a stronger assessment process. In estimating the time cost of assessment, institutions should be careful to include the time required for professional development and training, planning, engaging stakeholders, developing assessment tools, implementation, analysis and reporting. Colleagues who regularly conduct assessment and are strongly technically prepared are more likely (we state this with caution) to be able to quickly complete an assessment project—or, at least, to do so more quickly than those who are new to assessment or infrequently engage in the process.

Items to consider in developing appropriate time frames for assessment processes include:

- The level of development of and commitment to a project. Is the project ongoing, as in a yearly survey, or is an effort new to the organization? Has buy-in and opportunity for organizational commitment occurred, or will this need to be developed and nurtured? Have the assessment questions been framed? Has the purpose of the assessment been clearly determined?

Will the assessment use existing tools, or will it be necessary to develop new ones for gathering information?

What are the skills of the individuals who will be conducting the assessment? What is the level of preparedness of the organization? Do organizational or individual capacities to conduct assessment have to be further developed?

When will data collection occur? Not all times in an academic calendar are equally conducive to data gathering (e.g., summer, intersessions, and during finals or mid-terms).

The time required for data entry and analysis. It is important not to underestimate the time that transcribing, coding, and analyzing data takes. Data analysis in particular is a process that takes dedicated time and energy. Analysis is done more quickly by professionals who conduct analysis as part of their daily responsibilities, but, even then, the time required for analysis is likely to far exceed the time needed for data collection.

Both the time required for, and the timing of, reporting of assessment results. Collecting information that is not shared or utilized represents a major missed opportunity.

As a rule of thumb, assessment efforts should be considered in semester, year, and multi-year time frames, rather, than in periods of weeks or months. Promises to deliver a quality assessment effort in a tight time frame of a few weeks or months risk missed deadlines, invalid results, and the loss of overall support for ongoing assessment.

Other costs: Beyond human resources and time costs, there may be direct financial investments required, including:

The cost of obtaining and deploying specific assessment tools required for certain projects (e.g., surveys or software for data analysis).

Data gathering expenses (such as incentives to participate or travel to gather data).

Data entry or analysis expenses (including scanning, transcribing, and direct data entry, as well as any consultancy or outsourcing required for professional development, training, or data analysis).

Reporting expenses (including printing reports and web programming for electronic display of results, as examples).

Summary

The costs of assessment then can be expressed in dollars, new or repurposed human resources, time and the considerable commitment and energy necessary for developing and completing a process that attends to symbolic, political, human, and organizational elements. The complexity of conducting assessments with value (i.e., assessments that are valid, illuminating, and utilized) is perhaps seen most in the cost of lost opportunity. Assessments with value are opportunities to improve institutional effectiveness and student success. To under-resource assessment for short-term savings is, sadly and predictably, to invite and complete processes that fail to deliver on the promise of assessment because they lack time, sufficient expertise, adequate technical support, and enough organizational commitment to conduct an authentic, valuable process of inquiry that challenges the organization to engage in self-reflection, learn about its own work, and, ultimately, change based upon quality information that responds to the institution's core mission and values.

CHAPTER EIGHT

Framing Assessment Practice in Higher Education

The framing of assessment practice in higher education begins with understanding the variations among institutions and individuals that create a particular context for every college or university: institutional type, defined needs of learners, and organizational functioning. Colleges and universities are all unique because of variations in institutional types, diversity among learners, and differences in organizational structure and governance.

But first and foremost, framing assessment in higher education requires fitting the practice of assessment into institutions that, regardless of those variations, pride themselves on several key principles: academic freedom, self-governance, and the pursuit of knowledge. Inquiry into the activities of higher education must be completed with and through the organizational structures and core values of higher education, not in spite of those elements. Assessment should not be seen as a process through which external entities can *act upon* higher education, but rather a means by which systematically collected information can facilitate institutional reflection, renewal, and growth in response to a combination of internal commitments to improvement and societal calls for social and economic salience.

Internal and External Concerns

Assessment, in all its varied forms and approaches, is framed by the broad need for higher education to ensure its social, economic, and public salience, while at the same time maintaining its historical organizational independence and nature. The process of assessment in higher education always engages self-governance, affirms academic freedom, and strives to meaningfully inspire the institution to reflect upon the values that it directly espouses. The process of assessment is then an opportunity for the institution to attend to the needs of both internal and external constituents.

Institutional assessment practice is influenced by this need to address and balance external and internal constituent concerns. Institutions must attend to the demands of individuals, groups, and organizations who provide financial or other resources, and thus have a significant voice (e.g., funders, donors, accreditation groups, legislatures, employers) and also to groups that have less voice, but are nonetheless essential constituents (campus communities, public and private secondary schools, parents, and the amorphous public). Assessment efforts driven purely by external calls for information or demonstrations of accountability are likely to operate outside of organizational tenets of shared governance and thus are at serious risk for losing institutional cooperation and buy in (Zumeta, 2005). Similarly, assessment attention to only a few external constituents risks allowing assessment to be the tool of certain individuals with power to exert influence over organizational direction, either directly or subversively. Recent calls for attending to the public interest, or public good, of institutional functioning and performance suggest that higher education must instead engage questions of interest to a broad range of external constituents in the assessment process.

Similarly, there are internal constituents to whom assessment processes must attend, including senior leaders, administrators, faculty, professional staff, and students. Particular attention should be paid to colleagues within the institution who have less voice and are thus potentially less likely to be considered or addressed in an assessment process (notably including individuals from marginalized and historically underrepresented groups among students, faculty and staff; also, non-traditional students, part-time and adjunct or corporate faculty, and temporary staff). It is important to fit assessment into the organizational fabric of the campus in such a way that the process attends to and appreciates multiple constituents, rather than simply superimposing assessment onto the institution in an untailored, uncustomized fashion.

Assessment is, after all, a process of meaning making that should always include "reaching up," "reaching down," and "looking around." Assessment practice is directly informed by "reaching up"—that is, having an awareness of, and adapting to, the institution's mission, purpose and values—but also by "reaching down," to appreciate the details of the institution's footing, or context—attending to the institution's geographic and cultural roots, where it is located, what the needs and values of that city or region are, as well as who its students are, and what their particular learning and development needs embrace. "Looking around" informs assessment by ensuring that the practice of assessment is integrated and coordinated within and beyond departments and divisions and that assessment work is intertwined with the primary educational activities of the institution.

Fitting Assessment to Institutional Mission, Purpose, and Values

Assessment practice must be attentive to the context in which the institution operates. "Reaching up" includes, and indeed begins with, institutions' consideration of the contexts created by their governance—the state or community, especially, for public institutions, and the nation or region for both public and private schools, as well as spiritual tradition or authority for many universities; it then attends to the specific elements of institutional mission, vision, and values. The following list of factors points to variables to consider in assessment processes as those doing inquiry "reach up":

- Institutional mission, vision, direction, and values.

- Public or private governance.

- Religious affiliation (the influence of which varies within the category of religiously-affiliated institutions) or secular orientation.

- Institutional type (two-year, primarily undergraduate, liberal arts, regional comprehensive, or research intensive institution).

- Important institutional variations including tribal, Historically Black Colleges and Universities (HBCU), Hispanic Serving Institutions (HSI), or private for-profit.

Assessment needs and opportunities for an HBCU in the south or southeast are not the same as for an HSI in those regions or the southwest, nor for a for-profit institution operating in the northeast, a small Jesuit college in the Midwest, or a public institution in California. These differences are not simply geographic or typological; they reflect significant variations in mission, and, therefore, differences in the emphasis and range of intended student outcomes. To say assessment must be sensitive to those issues of context is, in some ways, the most obvious of statements—but it is relevant to the critical general point that assessment is never "one size fits all," and never done just for its own sake; assessment has key purposes for every type and location of institution, but the ways in which those purposes are addressed and operationalized will vary extensively.

Fitting Assessment to Student Needs

Equally, assessment must "reach down" and attend to the character, needs, and preferences of the institution's learners—and of the community, or region, in which the campus is located. "Reaching down" means responding to the historical and current roots of the institution—attending robustly and authentically to learners enrolled at a particular point in its life; it implies a deep institutional commitment to knowing students and their needs as those students and needs change over time. Why did this group of learners select the institution? What is it about them, and the school, that match? How does the curriculum link students' learning and developmental needs to the region and its challenges and opportunities?

Factors to consider in "reaching down" to frame assessment practice include:

- Ensuring that assessment processes recognize, include, and respond to the full diversity of learners present in the institution; especially, ensuring that assessment approaches hear the voices of students and employees who are members of groups that have been, and are, marginalized in an institution (i.e., underrepresented racial/ethnic groups, gay/lesbian/ transgendered individuals, students or faculty and staff members with disabilities, support staff).

- Understanding and applying learning outcomes that increase in developmental and cognitive complexity over the span of students' progression through the institution; that is, having a taxonomical approach.

- Modulating assessment approaches to fit both in- and out-of-class contexts for learning.

- Adapting assessment approaches to fit undergraduate, graduate, and professional school students.

- Reflecting how the institution is engaged in addressing community needs, such as workforce and economic development.

Locating Assessment in the Work of the Institution

"Looking around" is a strategy to ensure that assessment is a synthetic and organic part of the work of an institution, not a freestanding process or, worse, a hanging appendage. Factors to consider in "looking around" to frame assessment practice include:

- Making assessment within any division (such as student affairs) systematically integrated—that is, ensuring that the assessment work done by one department is somehow linked with, and reinforces, the assessment work done by others, and that, taken all together, the assessment activities of every department in the division describe the division's overall assessment commitments and goals. No department or individual should imagine that the assessment work they do is independent, isolated, or self-contained; assessment is, by nature, intersectional.

- Connecting assessment to certification and accreditation activities of professional preparation programs, such as those in medicine, physical therapy, athletic training, nursing, law, and business.

- Bringing a group of diverse individuals to the assessment table and taking stock of the disciplines they represent and talents they bring. The formation of an assessment team is a core component of a process of "looking around" to frame assessment practice. As noted in the previous chapter, creating an assessment team also involves taking inventory of institutional capacity in organizations and colleagues, and the overall ability of the institution to complete assessment activities.

- Determining what data exist, who holds it, how it can be accessed and utilized, and its validity is central to assessment work. Duplicating existing efforts is wasteful and undermines future support for further assessment efforts.

- Creating trans-divisional (truly institutional) assessment plans (by partnering student affairs educators with faculty members and administrators); similarly, creating ways to link and integrate assessment activities of all kinds planned or in place across campus.

Assessment practice is best conducted when it is framed by a clear understanding of how the activities of assessment can be completed as a webbed, or networked, collection of institutional processes working toward common objectives. Effective assessment requires good leadership practices across the institution that encourage and support the implementation of assessment in a coordinated, collaborative manner.

Summary

Assessment is framed by integrating processes of inquiry into the culture, governance, learners, and organizational relationships that exist in an institution. Often the path to meaningful assessment must be built upon an effort to build organizational assessment capacity. In fact, student affairs educators, faculty members, deans and other academic leaders, and administrators often share the journey of discovering how to conduct assessment in a given context—a context that is not shared in its exact details by any other institution. Locating assessment within institutional culture, values, and context is a strong way to avoid having it become just an unenthusiastic (and unproductive) response to external demands for accountability.

CHAPTER NINE

Assessment and Institutional Policy

Evidence from Peterson and Vaughan (2002) suggests that most institutions are engaged in some form of systematic assessment, but there remains a lingering question related to the extent, commitment, and integration of assessment into institutional policy making or revision. In fact, the unsettled question is not whether, but the extent to which, assessment should be integrated into institutional planning and policy. Strangely, the effectiveness of assessment as an institutional tool in planning and policy lacks significant evidence, to date, in the scholarship of higher education.

Current Practice: Assessment and Policy

Conceptually, the push toward assessment as a promising practice with which to tell the story of higher education, whether for accountability or improvement, seems readily accepted; this reflects a hopeful view of assessment, since broader evidence of the impact of inquiry in improving social programs (in areas other than higher education) is contested territory (Burke, 2005a). Although assessment activity in higher education has increased substantially since the late 1980s, one would be hard pressed to make the case that assessment has thus far had a causal effect in leading to strong, consistent, or significant improvements in student learning or institutional efficiency. Certainly there is little scholarly literature to suggest that sanguine conclusion. Many scholars, including the authors of this monograph, would hotly contest the suggestion that assessment as recently constructed in practice in higher education is primarily intended to enhance learning—or to lead to significant improvements in academic or experiential learning programs. A more realistic view is that current assessment practice primarily responds to external demands for accountability, and that the level, or intensity, of assessment effort is modulated to meet those demands—but not much more.

But the promise of assessment is in fact that an opportunity exists for organizational reflection, critique, and learning. At its best, assessment can be an opportunity to develop data for the purpose of aligning institutional vision, mission, and underlying values with practice; the assessment process is one that can facilitate and support on-going dialogue and provide data that encourages institutions to refine their purposes and policies. Most importantly, assessment has the real potential to be a tool with which to improve student learning.

The Potential of Assessment to Influence Institutional Policy

For assessment to be effective—to realize its potential—institutional policy toward assessment must do three things:

1. Ensure institutional integrity: pursue answers to the fundamental question, which is, do we walk our talk?

2. Provide evidence of learning (where learning is defined, as offered herein and in *Learning Reconsidered* (Keeling, 2004), as the integrated process of knowledge acquisition/application and development/social maturation).

3. Address questions of institutional policy and best practices: tight coupling of learning experiences; creating and sustaining purposeful horizontality across the institution; respecting, but not being restrained by, the vertical elements of institutional structure.

The pursuit of integrity in institutional policymaking is a demanding challenge for assessment. Developing information that richly responds to questions of institutional purpose, mission, and values demands significantly more of assessment practice than simply answering external calls for comparative information. There is strong evidence that the use of data is organizational decision making is mixed, complex, and muted by competing organizational factors (Patton, 1997). A commitment to the use of assessment in institutional policymaking requires the pursuit of information that has depth, perceived organizational validity, and practical application.

High quality outcomes data that are contextually appropriate becomes the minimum standard of practice for assessment professionals. An assessment process that responds to core institutional questions must develop evidence about student learning. Assessments of process are necessary but insufficient sources of information for institutional policymakers to use in making meaningful statements about learning. As noted in Chapter 7, assessing the outcomes of learning is costly, challenging, time intensive, and methodologically complicated, so leaders must be conscious that good evidence of student learning will require the investment of significant institutional resources.

Assessment has a special opportunity to attend to, and document, the horizontal, or cross-institutional, experience of engagement with the university (i.e., as a student would experience the institution, day to day). Data collected for that purpose provide evidence to share with the university community that will inform efforts to improve the nature and depth of student engagement. Connecting learning experiences through intention, rather than haphazardly, across courses, out-of-classroom learning opportunities, community service, library resources and activities, and virtual learning offerings should be broadly informed by an assessment process that considers how an institution's organization, or structure, is facilitating, or in fact detracting from, the achievement of key student learning goals. Assessment findings may prompt renewal or revision of the geographic, virtual, programmatic, and organizational relationships of learning experiences.

Organization of Assessment Activities

The process of advancing assessment to be an organizational practice that is relevant for institutional policy making is a process of ensuring that assessment is an integrated or organic, rather than add-on, practice. Institutions of higher education, as loosely coupled organizational systems, often assign responsibility for assessment to an administrative office or committee, or buy-out a portion of a faculty member's time to attend to the issue for the purpose of quality improvement, reporting, or self-study in preparation for accreditation. In some cases, organizations within an institution (e.g., divisions or large departments, and, in some smaller schools, the institution itself) have hired professionals to be in charge of assessment—a role that might include coordination of tasks, oversight of assessment practice, providing leadership and mentoring for colleagues, or leading particular institutional studies. A premise throughout this monograph has been to suggest a shift in how an organization approaches assessment leadership through which assessment practice is integrated, shared and culturally accepted.

An integrated view of the activities of assessment may still require allocated time in the forms of an administrative office, a portion of a faculty member's or student affairs professional's time, or a committee, but the roles of those entities change from responsibility for enacting assessment to leadership and coordination of varied and integrated assessment efforts operated throughout an institution. In the authors' view, colleges and universities err when they hire an assessment professional and expect that individual to manage or implement all institutional assessment activities.

Implications for Institutional Leadership

Institutional leadership, defined in the aggregate as the positions with responsibility and authority for decision-making, influence, and the exercise of institutional will and capacity must conceptualize assessment as a vehicle for bringing integrity to policy and practice. If institutional leaders see assessment as a necessary evil or a waste of time, little institutional renewal will occur. Leaders should embrace assessment as a strategy for reflecting on and responding to institutional identity, purpose, and functioning—not as a set of activities that appeases internal and external requirements.

Professional Development

Leadership must devote time and resources to planned, sustained, and intentional professional development. While it is popular to romanticize assessment practice as "easy," in reality, assessment practice is complex. Higher education professionals are most often content experts. Gaining expertise in learning, teaching, and assessment requires institutional commitment, will, and resources. Senior leadership—presidents, provosts, and vice-presidents must collaboratively develop unified visions and expectations for comprehensive assessment practice. The development of an assessment team cannot be a glib charge given to staff who are already engaged in multiple daily activities; assessment cannot be "tacked on."

Administrators, managers, and practitioners must hone their management skills so that comprehensive assessment practice is readily understood and embraced by their respective staffs. Working in harmony and engaging in regular discourse with senior leadership, high-level managers should provide adequate support and resources to bring vision and commitment to life. Communicating clear expectations, assignments, professional development, feedback loops, and realistic timelines can assuage anxiety and promote adoption of thoughtful, rigorous assessment practice.

A vital component of adopting credible assessment practice is developing a professional development curriculum. Senior leadership, managers, and practitioners will all benefit from crafting an institutional glossary, setting shared goals, engaging in thoughtful discussions, and practical didactic learning experiences that, experienced together, strengthen collegiality and assessment practice. A professional development curriculum should abide by principles of best practices; it should be planned, sequential, incorporate learning outcomes, respond to the variety of learning styles inherent in the institution, and itself, include credible assessment of learning.

Table 8 illustrates different professional development responsibilities for institutional leaders, administrators, managers, and practitioners.

Table 8. **Professional development in policy and practice.**

Senior Leadership	Administrators, Managers, and Practitioners
Develop and communicate a vision of comprehensive assessment practice that reflects the institution's mission, purpose, and commitment.	Develop a clear plan for institutionalizing comprehensive assessment practice
Create clear expectations.	Create regular opportunities for interdisciplinary staff to collaborate with one another and with key faculty members; develop assessment teams and charge them with specific tasks, timelines, and clear expectations.
Provide adequate fiscal, human, and technological resources for comprehensive assessment practice, including professional development.	Ensure that adequate resources are in place, that staff have the necessary knowledge and skills to fully engage in assigned tasks.
Charge management with developing a rewards and recognition system that motivates staff to present and publish not only assessment practices, but also lessons learned; promote best practices.	Implement a rewards and recognition systems. Assign presentation and publication as general job duties; advocate for sustained funding for sharing assessment practices, within and outside of the institution. Create leaders.

Comprehensive assessment practice that includes a well-crafted professional development curriculum brings the experience of learning full circle. Just as students are challenged to change their ways of knowing as a result of their engagement with their institution, so can leaders, managers, administrators, and practitioners gain new insight into their own ways of making meaning. This reflective practice adds depth, breadth and rigor to all aspects of higher education.

Programmatic Responsiveness

Informed, enlightened leaders can develop the capacity and skills to become *programmatically responsive.* This responsiveness must embrace a long-term approach to comprehensive assessment that includes cogent organizational goals about the parameters of change possible as a result of assessment findings. Effective leadership anticipates parameters of change. This means that leaders should commit to taking action based on assessment results, not personalities or history; programs that do not function as intended may be modified or eliminated, even if they are led by popular or long-serving professionals. The purposes of those programs may remain valid, however, so change may include professional development to build capacity to more effectively craft and deliver programs, realignment or renewal of existing talent, or creating new collaborations that draw greater advantage from other institutional talent. Assessment practice also often exposes hidden talent and highlights the levels of ability among staff and faculty to collaborate. It may illuminate professional development needs and identify cultural features of the institution that may have at one time been useful but have become non-functional or obsolete. Progressive, innovative leaders understand assessment practice, then, as more than a tactical response to external pressure; they see assessment as a tool that brings unity and a sense of identity and purpose to those charged with engaging in it. Assessment then becomes a solution-focused change management strategy. This allows leaders to be truly developmental—nurturing student success and collegial capacity—rather than remedial; that shift inspires a healthier workplace.

Implications for Parents, Alumni, and Community Stakeholders

Comprehensive student learning cannot be known, described, or documented without data that attest to its occurrence. Parents, alumni, and community stakeholders have begun to demand and expect more robust higher education experiences—by asking for more consistent, reproducible, and demonstrable outcomes that address societal, civic, and workforce needs. These expectations will be best met through a process of educating these important constituents about the purpose, mission, function, and outcomes of higher education. While mass media continue to have a prominent voice in shaping popular attitudes about the quality and success of higher education, it is now imperative that higher education professionals—those with expertise in the issues that are most important to the public—do exactly what they've been trained to do: educate. Assessment practice is a strong and important tool that can be used to thoughtfully educate the public about how higher education "works." Through the presentation of comprehensive student learning outcomes data, the public and higher education will find a partnership.

Summary

Assessment is complex, but higher education professionals and leaders have the ability to fully embrace it. The interdisciplinary nature of assessment allows higher education professionals to engage in meaningful discourse. Leaders can support assessment practice by providing professional development opportunities, supporting the allocation of sufficient time for the work to get done, and offering adequate technological resources for gathering, housing, and disseminating data.

CHAPTER TEN

Assessment Scholarship Reconsidered

Changes in science, education, political landscapes, the beliefs and expectations of communities, family and student demographics, technology, and the methods and pacing of communication have each and together opened up new windows through which to view and consider assessment scholarship. Postmodern perspectives, research paradigms, and cultural shifts offer rich and multiple frameworks to reconsider, re-imagine, and restructure assessment practice in higher education. These changes have important implications for higher education practice—both in the workplace and in the classrooms of future higher education professionals.

Implications for Graduate Professional Preparation Programs

What should the next generation of higher education professionals know, be able to do, and value in regard to assessment? Just as we challenge ourselves to align programs in such a way that students will reap the greatest possible *meaningful* benefit from them, we also must challenge ourselves to ensure that our graduate preparation programs in higher education provide meaningful benefit regarding assessment policy and practices for their students. There is a vital and immediate need for these graduate programs to develop cogent learning opportunities through which students who will be tomorrow's higher education professionals can develop the skills and competencies necessary to engage in comprehensive assessment practice.

Assessment should be an integrated component of graduate education programs—not just programs that prepare aspiring higher education administrators, but also in graduate education more generally.

First and foremost, graduate education should strive to model assessment as an integrated component of the educational process. We often teach as we were taught. Good teaching and learning in graduate professional programs begets good instructional leaders, just as bad teaching can beget poorly equipped educators. Modeling competent assessment practice in graduate education (including courses, practical experiences [i.e., labs, practica, and assistantships] as well as the overall course of study) is essential to advancing assessment through the next generations of student affairs administrators and disciplinary faculty members. Graduate faculty should ensure that assessment is an integrated cornerstone of their instructional pedagogy, whether through Web-enabled tests and surveys, in-class exercises, informal check-ins with advisees, or formal program evaluation.

Second, assessment should become an integrated learning component in the content of courses. Role modeling is one way that students can learn about assessment, but integrating key assessment content principles and concepts into graduate education is essential to ensuring that academic institutions have the professional capacity to address assessment challenges in the future. Fundamental assessment ideas including process and outcomes, primary methods, the thought process of assessment as a form of applied inquiry, and the use of basic tools to assess learning should be integrated components of coursework in all programs of graduate study. Within graduate programs focused on leadership in higher education, such as student affairs administration preparation programs, assessment should be a content area that has specific curricular attention.

Third, as the scholarship of the practice of assessment expands, students aspiring to be practitioners in higher education, or to teach in colleges and universities, should have specific content learning associated with a basic proficiency to consume and implement assessment efforts in postsecondary education. Basic educational research skills, frequently taught in survey courses associated with educational research, should be coupled with instruction that connects and differentiates educational research practice from assessment practice.

Implications for Contemporary Practitioners

In the table that follows, we explicate key implications of competency in assessment practice for practitioners in each of several professional areas in higher education.

Table 9. Implications for contemporary practice.

Profession	Implications for contemporary practice
Higher education leadership	• Develop a vision of comprehensive student learning experiences that clearly link classroom and experiential learning. • Provide leadership in the development of student affairs curricula, including comprehensive assessment planning. • Acquire and retain necessary human, fiscal, and technological resources to support comprehensive student learning.
Educational leadership	• Recruit and retain high quality talent to ensure rigor in comprehensive student learning programs, services, and systems of support. • Allocate resources in a manner that best matches student population assets and needs; move beyond stagnant practices that are based on convenience, history, or personalities. • Build staff and colleague readiness and capacity to fully embrace and engage in comprehensive student learning.
Counseling and college personnel	• Balance prevention, education, and remediation so that the developmental learning needs of all students are supported. • Move beyond measures of volume and satisfaction; strive for and implement programs that nurture academic, social, and intrapersonal maturity. • Work across disciplines so that students and colleagues experience a true universal experience rather than a collection of departments that work in parallel practice.
Student affairs practice	• Work and contribute as full partners in the mission of the institution. • Recognize and align core student affairs activities, such as residence life, student recreation, and student health as places and opportunities for students to develop important and necessary lifelong skills. • Mentor new generations of student affairs professionals to engage fully in comprehensive student learning including rigorous assessment practice.

Summary

Faculty, staff, administrators, and advanced graduate students can use lessons learned about assessment and institutional policy to make contributions to the professions that comprise higher education. The scholarship of higher education offers little meaningful, defensible literature that informs comprehensive assessment practice. The development, implementation, and publication of credible studies that advance the field of assessment of higher education is a challenge—but also an opportunity that obligates scholars, administrators, and educators.

CHAPTER ELEVEN

Assessment Results Reconsidered

In this final chapter, we draw together important themes from the preceding parts of the monograph to frame concluding thoughts and observations. The current context of higher education includes strong external pressures associated with the rising cost of tuition, concerns related to the workplace or professional competencies of graduates, and insistence on increasing the economic salience of higher education in the information age. Indeed, higher education is often described as a major engine in both workforce and economic development in a global marketplace where advanced skills and fluency in information technology are central to sustained economic growth and national prosperity. Attention to these questions of economic outcomes is prudent, but not sufficient, for those engaged in assessment in higher education; assessment must also consider how broader notions of the contributions of higher education to the public good are acknowledged, addressed, and documented.

Assessment of higher education, like higher education itself, is a practice of reflecting, learning, and making new knowledge upon which decisions can be made. Inquiry into the functioning of higher education must address issues and concerns beyond just organizational efficiency, operational effectiveness, student satisfaction, and market salience; the need for those measures, and for metrics like graduation rates, retention percentages, and key markers of basic professional skills (e.g., written and oral communication), must be augmented by indicators of institutional functioning pertinent to how an institution is informing pressing public debates, serving the community, developing the artistic appreciation of a new generation, and ensuring educational opportunity for the less privileged in society.

Making Assessment Salient

Assessment results then must be salient for a range of stakeholders who have diverse interests and agendas. There is no single approach, strategy, or grand survey that in and of itself can increase the overall salience of institutional assessment efforts. Rather, assessment is an engaged process of inquiry, rooted squarely in the political and symbolic values that are resolutely and unquestionably a part of the organization of higher education. With no magic bullets, what is left is the messiness of engaged inquiry, of multiple little steps that make up a practice of assessment. The process of making the results of assessment matter can be seen in the following list of approaches that, taken together, may help to weave a fabric of possibility that assessment can contribute to ensuring that higher education organizations are sustained as relevant social institutions in the future.

1. *The Purpose of Assessment Should Be Transparent*—Transparency is often used as a claim for assessment (assessment should strive to make clear the methods, means of analysis, and approach taken to ensure validity). While that understanding of transparency in assessment is important, transparency of purpose is a larger concept that refers to ensuring that assessment processes reveal their underlying intent, whether that purpose is to determine student needs (as in need analysis), judge the worth and value of programs, support making strategic decisions, market the institution to prospective students, work to develop new knowledge, seek to improve the institution, or aim to ensure that core institutional values are being upheld. Transparency of purpose requires clear knowledge of purpose as an absolute, unavoidable prerequisite (as obvious as that statement sounds, it does not reflect assessment practice in many contexts today). Knowledge of and openness about the purpose of assessment are important steps in creating a trustworthy, credible assessment process.

2. *A Culture of Assessment Matters More Than Projects*—Building a culture of assessment reflects an orientation toward organizational functioning

that is open to discovery, growth, and advancement. No single project defines assessment within an institution; rather, the overall effort toward engaging in critical examination of an institution's practices, outputs, and outcomes in the spirit of open discovery represents a sea-change in the culture of higher education. To create a culture that values, and in fact expects, faculty members and student affairs educators to examine their classroom or experiential learning practices and asks students to report on their learning is to create an optimal learning environment—a desirable aspiration for any institution.

3. *Assessment for, Rather Than of, Learning*—Too often, assessment seems to be in the business of speaking *about* whether learning occurred, rather than gathering information to assist in the processes of encouraging and supporting learning. While describing what has been learned is important for sharing the story of higher education, understanding how to better help students learn serves the vital institutional function of facilitating student learning and engagement. Assessment practices that promote learning should have just as much, or more, emphasis as those that seek to primarily measure learning and associated activities.

4. *Assessment as Engaged Practice*—Assessment can be seen as a component of engaged professional practice, rather than as owned and operated by a cadre of assessment experts. While experts and expertise are of course necessary for some aspects of assessment, the process of assessment is foundationally one of systematic inquiry that is a part of reflective professional practice for all campus educators. Institutions should strive to broadly develop the ability of faculty and student affairs professionals at all levels to be engaged assessment practitioners, or, better, scholar–practitioners, for whom systematic data collection in the spirit of action research, empowered evaluation, reflective practice, and engaged dialogue are commonplace (Erwin & Wise, 2002).

5. *Aligning Assessment with Aspirational (rather than "in practice") Institutional Values*—Colleges and universities have well crafted statements of purpose, mission, and vision that at their best reflect an institution's core values. Assessment practice should intentionally align itself with the aspirational values of an institution—not the "in practice" variations. Assessment practice, as it is rooted in applied social situations, is often quite practical in nature, and so runs the risk of operationalizing and lionizing "in practice" rather than aspirational values. An example

occurs in the selection of assessment methodology and implementation; when a survey method is selected for its pragmatic features, such as speed of delivery, cost effectiveness, and ease of analysis, the choice of method may have been made more in response to "in practice" values than true aspirational values that might point method selection toward ensuring a well-represented dialogue (which may still involve the use of a survey, but for different reasons).

6. *Making Reporting Matter*—Reporting of assessment efforts can best be seen as an integrated and on-going process of assessment, rather than simply an end-product (Patton, 1997). Reporting needs not take the form of simply a written report; alternative forms of reporting assessment results should be used to ensure that information is accessed, consumed, and becomes a part of the institutional decision-making and practice. Web-shared information, video segments, and podcasts of results—and more challenging reporting methods, such as data represented through art, are worth considering in certain contexts.

7. *Affirming the Use of Data*—There is ample evidence to suggest that the ultimate use of data in institutional decision-making is limited (Patton, 1997, for instance). Those who support the process of assessment must also engage in the regular practice of using data to support institutional decision-making. This is a challenge for instructors who use assessment to gauge classroom learning, the student affairs professional who assesses his or her favorite program and finds it lacking, and the senior administrator who learns from standardized test results that students are not achieving desired growth in critical thinking skills. Utilizing information to improve or change institutional decisions is an essential part of affirming the assessment data to make an institution more effective.

Preparing Assessment for the Future

One of the most promising opportunities for assessment is to be a part of sharing institutional performance stories from all types of higher education institutions. With the erosion of the implied public compact between higher education and society, in which there was great trust of higher education by society, new forms of responsiveness to the public's need for information about the activities of higher education are necessary. Assessment has the opportunity to be part of new ways of telling the performance story of higher education. There is, of course, risk to this opportunity. If the only assessment results that are shared are those that reflect simplistic measures or focus entirely on metrics associated with the economic contributions of higher education to society, then assessment risks being an agent of change that focuses institutional attention on activities and effects that are closest to the economy potentially—likely at the expense of universities' activities that contribute in humanistic ways (Ehrenberg, 2002).

If assessment is to progress from a fledgling response to external calls for accountability to a sophisticated practice that reflects the complexity of higher education, it must find its own voice (Ewell, 2002). Assessment that simply answers demands from external constituents for greater accountability is not progress; it represents just a new layer of distraction away from the engaging conversations that must occur as institutions push and pull toward and against responsiveness to and resistance of social, political, and economic changes in society (Alexander, 2002). Part of the strength of higher education has not only been its continuing relevance in pursuing and disseminating knowledge that addresses social and economic issues in society, but also its persistence and sustainability as a repository of knowledge, keeper of tradition, and strong institution in society (Alexander, 2002).

The business of assessment, then, is the business of the university itself. The institution has a responsibility to share its story with the public, which contributes so strongly to its financial viability through tax support, charitable contributions, and student tuition. Assessment of, and for, learning reflects the broad and universally accepted institutional purpose of assisting students in their learning and development.

REFERENCES

Agresti, A. & Fnlay, B. (1997). *Statistical methods for the social sciences* (3rd edition). New Jersey: Prentice Hall.

Ajzen, I. (1985). From intentions to actions: A theory of planned behavior. In J. Kuhl & J. Beckman (Eds.), *Action-control: From cognition to behavior* (pp. 11–39). Heidelberg: Springer.

Alexander, J.M. & Stark, J.S. (2003). Focusing on student academic outcomes. In W.Y. Lee (Ed.), *ASHE reader series: Assessment and program evaluation* (2nd edition, pp. 349–356). Boston: Pearson Custom Publishing.

Alexander, K. (2002). The object of the university: Motives and motivations. In F.K. Alexander & K. Alexander (Eds.), *The university: International expectations* (pp. 3–20). Ithaca: McGill-Queen's University Press.

Alexander, F. (2002). Financing university performance in Britain and the United States. In F.K. Alexander & K. Alexander (Eds.), *The university: International expectations* (pp.69–80). Ithaca: McGill-Queen's University Press.

Altheide, D.L. & Johnson, J.M. (1998). Criteria for assessing interpretive validity in qualitative research. In N.K. Denzin & Y.S. Guba (Eds.), *Collecting and interpreting qualitative materials* (pp. 283–312). Thousand Oaks, CA: Sage Publications.

Angelo, T.A. (2002). Engaging and supporting faculty in the scholarship of assessment: Guidelines from research and best practice. In T.W. Banta & Associates (Eds.), *Building a scholarship of assessment* (pp. 185–200). San Francisco: Jossey-Bass.

Banta, T.W. (2002). Characteristics of effective outcomes assessment: Foundations and examples. In T.W. Banta & Associates (Eds.), *Building a scholarship of assessment* (pp. 261–283). San Francisco: Jossey-Bass.

Banta, T.W. (2002a). A call for transformation. In T.W. Banta & Associates (Eds.), *Building a scholarship of assessment* (pp. 284–292). San Francisco: Jossey-Bass.

Banta, T.W. (2003). Contemporary approaches to assessing student achievement of general education outcomes. In W.Y. Lee (Ed.), *ASHE reader series: Assessment and program evaluation* (2nd edition, pp. 357–368). Boston: Pearson Custom Publishing.

Baumrind, D. (1989). Rearing competent children. In W. Damon (Ed.), *Child development today and tomorrow.* San Francisco: Jossey-Bass.

Bennett, M., Dennett, D., Hacker, P., & Searle, J. (2007). Neuroscience & philosophy: brain, mind, & language. New York: Columbia University Press.

Black, K.E. & Kline, K.A. (2002). Program review: A spectrum of perspectives and practices. In T.W. Banta & Associates (Eds.), *Building a scholarship of assessment* (pp. 223–239). San Francisco: Jossey-Bass.

Bloom, B.S. (1956). *Taxonomy of Educational Objectives, Handbook I: Cognitive Domain.* New York: Longman, Green.

Bloom, R.S. (1975). Stating Educational Objectives in Behavioral Terms. *Nursing Forum* 14(1), 31–42.

Borden, V.M.H. (2002). Information support for assessment. In T.W. Banta & Associates (Eds.), *Building a scholarship of assessment* (pp. 167–182). San Francisco: Jossey-Bass.

Burke, J.C. & Associates (Eds.). (2005). *Achieving accountability in higher education.* San Francisco: Jossey-Bass.

Burke, J.C. (2005a). The many faces of accountability. In J.C. Burke & Associates (Eds.), *Achieving accountability in higher education* (pp. 1–24). San Francisco: Jossey-Bass.

Burke, J.C. (2005b). Reinventing accountability: From bureaucratic rules to performance results. In J.C. Burke & Associates (Eds.), *Achieving accountability in higher education* (pp. 216–245). San Francisco: Jossey-Bass.

Christians, C.G. (2003). Ethics and politics in qualitative research. In N.K. Denzin & Y.S. Lincoln (Eds.), *The landscape of qualitative research: Theories and issues.* (2nd edition, pp. 208-244). Thousand Oaks, CA: Sage Publications.

Chickering, A.W. & Reisser, L. (1993). *Education and identity* (2nd edition). San Francisco: Jossey-Bass.

Cohon, A.M. (1998*). The Shaping of American Higher Education.* San Fransicso: Jossey-Bass.

Creswell, J.W. (1997). Qualitative Inquiry and Research Design: Choosing Among Five Traditions. Thousand Oaks, CA: Sage Publications.

Creswell, J.W., Plano Clark, V.L., Gutmann, M.L. & Hanson, W.E. (2003). Advanced mixed methods research designs. In A. Tashakkori & C. Teddlie (Eds.), *Handbook of mixed methods in social and behavioral research* (pp. 209–240). Thousand Oaks, CA: Sage Publications.

Davis, B.G. (2003). Demystifying assessment: Learning from the field of evaluation. In W.Y. Lee (Ed.), *ASHE reader series: Assessment and program evaluation* (2nd edition, pp. 33–44). Boston: Pearson Custom Publishing.

Dean, L.A. (2006). CAS Professional Standards for Higher Education (6th edition). Washington DC: Council for the Advancement of Standards in Higher Education.

Denzin, N.K. & Lincoln, Y.S. (Eds.). (2003). *The landscape of qualitative research: Theories and issues.* (2nd edition). Thousand Oaks, CA: Sage Publications.

Denzin, N.K. & Lincoln, Y.S. (2003a). Introduction: The discipline and practice of qualitative research. In N.K. Denzin & Y.S. Lincoln (Eds.), *The landscape of qualitative research: Theories and issues* (2nd edition, pp.1–46). Thousand Oaks, CA: Sage Publications.

Ehrenberg, R. G. (2000). *Tuition rising: Why college costs so much.* Boston: Harvard University Press.

Erwin, T.D. & Wise, S.L. (2002). A scholar-practitioner model for assessment. In T.W. Banta & Associates (Eds.), *Building a scholarship of assessment* (pp. 67–81). San Francisco: Jossey-Bass.

Evans, N.J., Forney, D.S., & Guido-DiBrito, F. (1998). *Student development in college: Theory, research, and practice.* San Francisco: Jossey-Bass.

Ewell, P.T. (2002). An emerging scholarship: A brief history of assessment. In T.W. Banta & Associates (Eds.), *Building a scholarship of assessment* (pp. 3–25). San Francisco: Jossey-Bass.

Ewell, P.T. (2005). Can assessment serve accountability? It depends on the question. In J.C. Burke & Associates (Eds.), *Achieving accountability in higher education* (pp. 104–124). San Francisco: Jossey-Bass.

Fetro, J.V. (1998). *Step by step to health promoting schools: A guide to implementing coordinated school health programs in local schools and districts.* Santa Cruz, CA: ETR Associates.

Fetro, J.V. & Drolet, J.C. (2000). *Personal & social competence: Strategies for communication, decision making, goal setting, stress management.* Santa Cruz, CA: ETR Associates.

Gall, M.D., Gall, J.P. & Borg, W.R. (2003). *Educational research: An introduction* (7th edition). Boston: Pearson Education, Inc.

Gardner, D.E. (2003). Five evaluation frameworks: Implications for decision making in higher education. In W.Y. Lee (Ed.), *ASHE reader series: Assessment and program evaluation* (2nd edition, pp. 5–18). Boston: Pearson Custom Publishing.

Gladwell, M. (2000). *The Tipping Point: How Little Things Can Make a Big Difference.* New York: Little, Brown.

Glanz, K. (1997). Community and group intervention models of health behavior change. In K. Glanz, F.M. Lewis, & B.K. Rimer (Eds.), *Health behavior and health education: Theory, practice and research* (2nd edition, pp. 237–239). San Francisco: Jossey-Bass.

Gray, P.J. (2002). The roots of assessment: Tensions, solutions, and research directions. In T.W. Banta & Associates (Eds.), *Building a scholarship of assessment* (pp. 49-66). San Francisco: Jossey-Bass.

Greene, J.C., Caracelli, V.J., & Graham, W.F. (1989). Toward a Conceptual Framework for Mixed Method Evaluation Designs. *Educational Evaluation and Policy Analysis, 2*(3), 255–274.

Greene, J.C. & Caracelli, V.J. (2003). Making paradigmatic sense of mixed methods practice. In A. Tashakkori & C. Teddlie (Eds.), *Handbook of mixed methods in social and behavioral research* (pp. 91–110). Thousand Oaks, CA: Sage Publications.

Greenwood, D. & Levin, M. (2003). Reconstructing the relationships between universities and society through action research. In N.K. Denzin & Y.S. Lincoln (Eds.), *The landscape of qualitative research: Theories and issues* (2nd edition, pp. 131–166). Thousand Oaks, CA: Sage Publications.

Gronlund, N.E. (1970). *Stating behavioral objectives for classroom instruction.* New York: Macmillan.

Harrow, A. (1972). A taxonomy of the psychomotor domain: A guide for developing behavioral objectives. New York: McKay.

House, E.R. & Howe, K.R. (2000). Deliberative democratic evaluation. *New Directions for Evaluation, 85,* 3–12

Isaac, S. & Michael, W.B. (1997). *Handbook in research and evaluation: For educational and the behavioral sciences.* San Diego, CA: Educational and Industrial Testing Services.

Johnson, R.B. & Onwuegbuzie, A.J. (2004). Mixed methods research: A research paradigm whose time has come. *Educational Researcher, 33(7),* 14–26.

Joint Committee on Standards for Educational Evaluation. (1994). *The program evaluation standards: How to assess evaluations of educational programs* (2nd edition). Thousand Oaks, CA: Sage Publications.

Jonassen, D., Hannum, W. & Tessmer, M. (1989). Bloom's taxonomy of educational objectives. *Handbook of task analysis procedures* (Chapter 12). New York: Praeger.

Keeling, R.P. (Ed.). (2004). *Learning Reconsidered: A Campuswide Focus on the Student Experience.* Washington, DC: American College Personnel Association and National Association of Student Personnel Administrators.

Keeling, R.P. (Ed.). (2006). *Learning Reconsidered 2: Implementing a Campuswide Focus on the Student Experience.* Washington, DC: National Association of Student Personnel Administrators, American College Personnel Association, and five other associations.

Keeling, R.P., Underhile, R., Wall, A.F. (2007). Horizontal and vertical structures: The dynamics of organization in higher education. *Liberal Education*, 93(4), 22–31.

Kezar, A.J.; Chambers, T.C.; Burkhardt, J.C. & Associates. (2005). *Higher education for the public good: Emerging voices from a national movement.* San Francisco: Jossey-Bass.

Kuh, G.D., Gonyea, R.M. & Rodriguez, D.P. (2002). The scholarly assessment of student development. In T.W. Banta & Associates (Eds.), *Building a scholarship of assessment* (pp. 100–128). San Francisco: Jossey-Bass.

Kuzma, J.W. & Bohnenblust, S.E. (2001). *Basic statistics for the health sciences* (4th edition). Boston: McGraw-Hill.

Lee, W.Y. (Ed.). (2003). *ASHE reader series: Assessment and program evaluation* (2nd edition). Boston: Pearson Custom Publishing.

Lewin, K. (1951). *Field theory in social science: Selected theoretical papers.* New York: Harper & Row.

Lincoln, Y.S. & Guba, E.G. (2003). But is it rigorous? Trustworthiness and authenticity in naturalistic evaluation. In W.Y. Lee (Ed.), *ASHE reader series: Assessment and program evaluation* (2nd edition, pp. 643–650). Boston: Pearson Custom Publishing.

Madaus, G.F.; Stufflebeam, D. & Scriven, M.S. (2003) Program evaluation: A historical overview. In W.Y. Lee (Ed.), *ASHE reader series: Assessment and program evaluation* (2nd edition, pp.19–32). Boston: Pearson Custom Publishing.

Maslow, A. H. (1971). *The farther reaches of human nature.* New York: Viking.

Mentkowski, M. & Loacker, G. (2002). Enacting a collaborative scholarship of assessment.

In T.W. Banta & Associates (Eds.), *Building a scholarship of assessment* (pp. 82–99). San Francisco: Jossey-Bass.

Messick, S. (2003). The changing face of higher education assessment. In W.Y. Lee (Ed.), *ASHE reader series: Assessment and program evaluation* (2nd edition, pp. 45–48). Boston: Pearson Custom Publishing.

O'Banion, T. (1999). *Launching a learning-centered colleges.* League for Innovation in the Community College.

Onwuegbuzie, A.J. & Teddlie, C. (2003). A framework for analyzing data in mixed methods research. In A. Tashakkori & C. Teddlie (Eds.), *Handbook of mixed methods in social and behavioral research* (pp. 351–384). Thousand Oaks, CA: Sage Publications.

Palomba, C.A. (2002). Scholarly assessment of student learning in the major and general education. In T.W. Banta & Associates (Eds.), *Building a scholarship of assessment* (pp. 201–222). San Francisco: Jossey-Bass.

Palomba, C.A. & Banta, T.W. (2003). Encouraging involvement in assessment. In W.Y. Lee (Ed.), *ASHE reader series: Assessment and program evaluation* (2nd edition, pp. 113–128). Boston: Pearson Custom Publishing.

Palomba, C.A. & Banta, T.W. (1999). *Assessment essentials: Planning, implementing, and improving assessment in higher education.* San Francisco: Jossey-Bass.

Patton, L. (1997). *Utilization Focused Evaluation.* Thousand Oaks: Sage Publications.

Peterson, M.W. & Vaughan, D.S. (2002). Promoting academic improvement: Organizational and administrative dynamics that support student assessment. In Banta, T.W. (Ed.), Building A Scholarship of Assessment. San Francisco: Jossey-Bass.

Pike, G.R. (2002). Measurement issues in outcomes assessment. In T.W. Banta & Associates (Eds.), *Building a scholarship of assessment* (pp.131–147). San Francisco: Jossey-Bass.

Piper, T. (2007). In Search of the Wizard of Assessment. *About Campus, 12*(5), 24–27.

Pittman, K. & Cahill, M. (1992). *Pushing the boundaries of education: The implication of a youth development approach to education policies, structures, and collaborations.* Washington, DC: Center for Youth Development and Policy Research, Academy for Educational Development.

Posavac, E.J. & Carey, R.G. (1997). *Program evaluation: Methods and case studies* (5th edition). Upper Saddle River, NJ: Prentice-Hall, Inc.

Prochaska, J.O. & DiClemente, C.C. (1984). *The transtheoretical approach: Crossing traditional boundaries of therapy.* Homewood, IL: Dow Jones-Irwin.

Ramaley, J.A. (2005). Scholarship for the public good: Living in Pasteur's Quadrant. In A.J. Kezar, T.C. Chambers, J.C. Burkhardt & Associates (Eds.), *Higher education for the public good: Emerging voices from a national movement.* San Francisco: Jossey-Bass.

Rocco, T.S., Bliss, L.A., Gallagher, S., Perez-Prado, A., Alacaci, C., Dwyer, E.S., et al. (2003). The pragmatic and dialectical lenses: Two views of mixed methods use in education. In A. Tashakkori & C. Teddlie (Eds.), *Handbook of mixed methods in social and behavioral research* (pp. 577–594). Thousand Oaks, CA: Sage Publications.

Rogers, E. M. (1995). *Diffusion of innovations* (4th edition). New York: Free Press.

Rothman, J. (1968) Three models of community organization practice in *Social Work Practice 1968.* New York: Columbia University Press.

Schwandt, T.A. (1996). Farewell to criteriology. *Qualitative Inquiry, 2,* 58–72.

Schwandt, T.A. (2003). Three epistemological stances for qualitative inquiry: Interpretivism, hermeneutics, and social constructionism. In N.K. Denzin & Y.S. Lincoln (Eds.), The landscape of qualitative research: Theories and issues. (2nd edition, pp. 292–331). Thousand Oaks, CA: Sage Publications.

Sell, G.R. (2003). An organizational perspective for the effective practice of assessment. In W.Y. Lee (Ed.), ASHE reader series: Assessment and program evaluation (2nd edition, pp. 95–108). Boston: Pearson Custom Publishing.

Sewall, A.M. & Smith, T.E.C. (2003). Effective and ineffective assessment programs in higher education. In W.Y. Lee (Ed.), ASHE reader series: Assessment and program evaluation (2nd edition, pp.129–132). Boston: Pearson Custom Publishing.

Shermis, M.D. & Daniels, K.E. (2002). Web applications in assessment. In T.W. Banta & Associates (Eds.), Building a scholarship of assessment (pp. 148–166). San Francisco: Jossey-Bass.

Shulman, L. (2007). Keynote Address AAC&U. AAC&U National Conference: New Orleans, LA.

Strauss, A. & Corbin, J. (1998). Basics of qualitative research: Techniques and procedures for developing grounded theory (2nd edition). Thousand Oaks, CA: Sage Publications.

Stufflebeam, D.L. & Shinkfield, A. J. (1985). *Systematic evaluation: A self-instructional guide to theory and practice.* Hingham, MA: Kluwer-Nijoff.

Tashakkori, A. & Teddlie, C. (Eds.). (2003). *Handbook of mixed methods in social and behavioral research*. Thousand Oaks, CA: Sage Publications.

Teddlie, C. & Tashakkori, A. (2003). Major issues and controversies in the use of mixed methods in the social and behavioral sciences. In A. Tashakkori & C. Teddlie (Eds.), *Handbook of mixed methods in social and behavioral research* (pp. 3–50). Thousand Oaks, CA: Sage Publications.

U.S. Department of Health and Human Services, National Institute of Health (2005). Theory at a Glance: Application to Health Promotion and Health Behavior (2nd edition).

Vidich, A.J. & Lyman, S.M. (2003). Qualitative methods: Their history in sociology and anthropology. In N.K. Denzin & Y.S. Lincoln (Eds.), *The landscape of qualitative research: Theories and issues* (2nd edition, pp. 55–130). Thousand Oaks, CA: Sage Publications.

Whitt, E.J. (1999). Student learning and student affairs work: Responding to our imperative. Washington, DC: National Association of Student Personnel Administrators.

Wright, B.D. (2002). Accreditation and the scholarship of assessment. In T.W. Banta & Associates (Eds.), *Building a scholarship of assessment* (pp. 240–258). San Francisco: Jossey-Bass.

Zumeta, W.M. (2005). Accountability in the private sector: State and federal perspectives. In J.C. Burke & Associates (Eds.), *Achieving accountability in higher education* (pp. 25–54). San Francisco: Jossey-Bass.

ABOUT THE AUTHORS

RICHARD P. KEELING, M.D., is Principal and Senior Executive Consultant for Keeling & Associates, LLC, Co-Founder of the International Center for Student Success and Institutional Accountability (ICSSIA), and Editor of both *Learning Reconsidered* and *Learning Reconsidered 2*.

ANDREW F. WALL, PH.D., is Assistant Professor in the Warner Graduate School of Education and Human Development at the University of Rochester and serves as a Senior Consultant for Keeling & Associates, LLC.

RIC UNDERHILE, PH.D., is Senior Consultant for Keeling & Associates, LLC; he designs capacity building and professional development curricula for leadership in institutions of higher education.

GWENDOLYN J. DUNGY, PH.D., is Executive Director of the National Association of Student Personnel Administrators (NASPA) and Co-Founder of the International Center for Student Success and Institutional Accountability (ICSSIA).

ACKNOWLEDGMENTS

The authors acknowledge with great appreciation the work of Augustine P. Bartning, Director of Institutional and International Strategies for Keeling & Associates, who served as managing editor; and Melissa Dahne, Director of Publications for NASPA, who served as production manager for this project.